Wonderful Rooms
Where Children Can Bloom!

————————●————————

Also Available from Crystal Springs Books

Building Number Sense
Differentiated Math
Morning Meeting, Afternoon Wrap-Up
Poems for Sight-Word Practice
You Can't Teach a Class You Can't Manage

————————●————————

Other Books by Jean R. Feldman, PhD

Best of Dr. Jean: Hands-On Art
Best of Dr. Jean: Puppets & Storytime
Best of Dr. Jean: Reading & Writing
Best of Dr. Jean: Science & Math
Rainy Day Activities
Ready-to-Use Self Esteem Activities for Young Children
Transition Time
Transition Tips & Tricks

Wonderful Rooms

Where Children Can Bloom!

Over 500 Innovative Ideas and Activities for Your Child-Centered Classroom

Jean R. Feldman, PhD

SDE Crystal Springs BOOKS

a division of Staff Development for Educators
Peterborough, New Hampshire

Published by Crystal Springs Books
A division of Staff Development for Educators (SDE)
10 Sharon Road, PO Box 500
Peterborough, NH 03458
1-800-321-0401
www.SDE.com/crystalsprings

© 2011 Jean R. Feldman
Illustrations © 2011 Crystal Springs Books

Published 2011
Printed in the United States of America
15 14 13 12 11   1 2 3 4 5

ISBN: 978-1-935502-07-4

Library of Congress Cataloging-in-Publication Data

Feldman, Jean R., 1947-
    Wonderful rooms where children can bloom! : over 500 innovative ideas and
    activities for your child-centered classroom / by Jean R. Feldman. -- [2nd ed.].
    p. cm.
ISBN 978-1-935502-07-4
1. Education, Primary--Activity programs. 2. Classroom learning centers.
3. Classrooms. I. Title.
LB1537.F46   2011
371.24'1--dc23
                              2011022156

Art Director and Designer: Bill Smith Group
Cover Design: Bill Smith Group
Production Coordinator: Deborah Fredericks
Illustrations: S. Dunholter and Q2A Media

This book is dedicated to

Frances Bethel,
My friend and department chair
for many years. Thanks for
encouraging me and giving me
a job where I could grow!

Acknowledgments

"Soup from a stone, fancy that!!" Remember how everyone contributed to make the wonderful soup in the folk tale, *Stone Soup*? So it is with *Wonderful Rooms*, in which so many teachers have shared their creative ideas for helping children grow.

To all of you I say, "Thank you!" And the teachers who use this book as a resource, and the children whose lives are touched in a small way because of those ideas, will say, "Thank you," too!

Contents

Share The Wonder!

Surround children in beauty.

Embrace them with love each day.

Share their wonder of discovery.

Share their joy as they play.

Help children be successful.

Make them feel special, too.

With choices and hands-on learning,

They'll grow and learn as they do!

Give children peace and happy memories.

Create warm and inviting rooms.

Cherish all of the children.

And they will surely bloom!

There is a powerful relationship between environment and behavior. If we want children to feel comfortable, confident, secure, and happy, then we must create beautiful schools where they can grow and develop to their fullest potential. In a world where children spend more waking hours in school than they do in their own homes, the need to provide them with warm, nurturing spaces is particularly important.

This book shows you how to create these nurturing environments, in your school and in your classroom. Part 1 gives you ways of making your whole school an inviting place for your children and their parents, inside and out. Part 2 takes you inside your classroom, giving you many ideas on making your physical space attractive. This section also deals with such practical matters as portfolios and teacher storage tips.

Part 3 tells you how to create a literate environment. Part 4 shows you ways to use your children's art as a main focus in planning your room.

Learning centers are invaluable in creating a child-centered environment. Part 5 is devoted entirely to learning centers, providing management and documentation tips as well as lots of ideas for creative, fun activities in a number of different centers.

Children learn by playing. Part 6 gives you many games that will challenge your children's minds and build their skills while letting them have fun.

Wonderful Rooms Where Children Can Bloom! is meant to be a resource for creating a meaningful and dynamic classroom where all children can grow in their own unique ways. These ideas can easily be adapted to reflect the personalities of your children, community, and program. It is a challenge and it is work, but children are worthy of the most beautiful, happy, loving, and exciting schools we can give them!

PART 1

In, Out, and About

Ideas for Enhancing the Ambiance of Your School

Little things count—little children, and all the little things you do in your school to create an effective learning environment. This chapter will offer you ideas for:

- ▶ landscaping and road appeal
- ▶ inviting lobbies
- ▶ a parent resource center
- ▶ playground fun

Out Front – Road Appeal

How your school looks from the road reflects your philosophy and what's happening inside. Check these out:

▶ Drive past your school. What kind of first impression would it give to others?

▶ Is there an attractive sign with your school's name?

▶ What is the landscaping like? Are the bushes trimmed? Is the curb manicured and free of debris? Is the grass well maintained?

▶ Are the driveway and sidewalks clean and in good repair?

▶ Is the building well cared for?

Try these ideas!

▶ Let children plant flower beds in the front of the school, or use decorative pots of flowers by the front door.

▶ Use seasonal displays, such as pumpkins, scarecrows, a flag, or wreaths.

▶ Put a welcome mat by the front door.

Lovely Lobbies

The lobby gives a first and lasting impression of your school. These ideas will create a warm ambiance.

Senses
How does your lobby smell when you enter the school? Fresh flowers, plants, air fresheners, or potpourri can add pleasant odors.

Do you hear the happy sounds of children? The sound of children's music or a recording of your students singing is more positive than commercial radio stations.

Is the entrance sunny and well-lit? Window treatments, a comfortable seating arrangement, pillows, and children's art will create a positive, home-like environment. Rather than hanging adult art and posters, use pictures, murals, and three-dimensional projects created by the children in your school.

News
Use an easel or dry-erase board in the lobby to remind parents of schedule changes, special events, and other news. If a computer monitor is mounted in the lobby, it can be used to display news.

Input
A suggestion box will let parents know you value their ideas.

Album
Keep a photo album in your lobby with up-to-date pictures of all the activities in your school. Also, capture field trips, parties, and other special moments. Children and parents will enjoy recalling memories as they look at the album. If a computer monitor is available, display a slide show of school photos. The monitor can also be used to share videos of the children in action. (Remember to get parental permission before displaying photos of children.)

Family Tree   Ask each family to bring in a family photograph. Glue the photos to construction paper cut in geometric or seasonal shapes (leaves in the fall, flowers in the spring, etc.). Punch a hole in the ornaments and tie them onto a plant or artificial tree with ribbons.

VIP Family   Choose a family each week to highlight, and make a poster to display in the lobby. Include pictures of family members and pets, and information on hobbies, favorite foods, things they enjoy doing together, etc.

The Parents' Place

The role of parenting can be supported by a resource library in your school.

Materials
☐ parenting books (ages and stages, discipline, sibling rivalry, etc.)

☐ pertinent articles on parenting (bedtime, ADHD, single parenting, health issues, etc.)

☐ audio CDs and DVDs on parenting topics

☐ lists of recommended online resources for specific subject areas and for specific ages and stages of development

☐ bookshelf, table

☐ comfortable chairs

Directions Place the books, CDs, and DVDs on a shelf in your lobby. Articles can be organized by topic and stored in a file box. Have parents sign out materials. Photocopies of online resource lists can be organized by topic and made available for parents to take home as needed.

Variations Encourage parents to add to the resource center by sharing books or articles that have been helpful to them.

Create an eye-catcher for children in the lobby, too. It might be an aquarium, a school mascot (a large stuffed animal), a Big Book display, an antique school desk, or a box sculpture designed by children.

Outdoor Fun

Care and planning should also be devoted to the outdoor play area. Besides having fun, children develop important social, language, motor, and emotional skills as they play outside.

Enchanted Garden

Materials
- ☐ garden spot
- ☐ child-sized garden plants
- ☐ seeds or bedding plants
- ☐ large rocks
- ☐ waterproof paints, old brushes

Directions Involve the children in preparing the soil by letting them dig in the dirt several days prior to planting the garden. Let them decide what flowers they would like to plant, and guide them in planting the seeds. Help children find large rocks and paint them, then outline the garden with the rocks. Encourage the children to take responsibility for watering the garden, pulling the weeds, etc.

Variations Use tubs, planters, or old tires for a garden.

Plant vegetable seeds that the children can harvest and eat. Call it your "soup garden."

Plant flowers in colorful rows to resemble a rainbow, or plant red, white, and blue flowers in the shape of a flag.

Music in the Air

Materials
- ☐ bells, wind chimes
- ☐ ribbon or string

Directions Tie old bells or wind chimes to the branches of a tree with ribbon or string. When the wind blows, the tree will sing to you.

Fitness Trail

Materials ☐ poster board ☐ clear contact paper
☐ markers ☐ string

Directions Involve the children in creating a fitness trail for the playground. It might include doing jumping jacks, going down the slide, climbing a pole, riding a tricycle, etc. Let them number the activities, write the directions, and draw pictures on the poster board. Cover with clear contact paper, then use string to tie at different points on the playground.

Road Trip

Materials ☐ copy paper
☐ computer
☐ digital camera
☐ glue
☐ scissors

Directions During outdoor time, have scooters, tricycles, and other riding toys available for children to use. Children must know the school's "rules of the road" before they can start riding. After teaching the rules to children, have them "apply" for a driver's license. Give each child who learns the rules of the road their own license.

Create the driver's license on the computer or by hand and photocopy one per child. Have each child recite his name, address, and birthday while you write it on the driver's license. Take a photo of each child (preferably a head shot) with the digital camera. Print out each child's photo, cut it out, and glue it to the driver's license.

Variation Instead of taking photos of the children, have them draw self-portraits for their driver's licenses.

Sidewalk Fun

Materials ☐ sidewalk paint
☐ old brushes

Directions Design different objects and games that you can paint on your sidewalk. You might do foursquare, hopscotch, geometric shapes, silly footprints to follow, road signs, etc.

Roll-a-Rama

Materials ☐ clear plastic pipe (4'–10')
☐ duct tape
☐ small cars, balls, or toys

Directions Tape the pipe to the fence at an angle. Children can put the toys in the top end and watch them roll out the bottom.

Variations Have children put toys into cardboard tubes so they can watch them roll out the other end. Use different-sized tubes from wrapping paper, laminating film, carpet, and fabric.

Purchase plastic drain pipes at a hardware store and use in a similar manner.

STEP IT UP Have children test the effects of different types of tubes and different inclines on speed. Have children use stopwatches to time how fast their toys travel to the bottom of different tubes set at different inclines. Ask children to write about what they observed.

Windsocks and Pinwheels

Materials ☐ windsocks, pinwheels, banners, and flags

Directions Attach windsocks, pinwheels, flags, and banners to fences and trees on the playground. As you discuss the weather with children, encourage them to explain how windsocks, pinwheels, and flags provide details about the weather.

Variation Let the children make the flags and banners with old sheets and markers.

Nature Center

Materials ☐ bird feeders
☐ rocks, trees, bushes, and natural items

Directions Create your own nature center with feeders, plants, a rock garden, etc.

alkie Talkie

Materials
- [ ] 2 plastic funnels
- [ ] 6'–8' clear tubing (size the tubing to fit into the ends of the funnels)
- [ ] duct tape

Directions Tape a funnel to each end of the tubing. Put one funnel at the top of a playground climber. Use duct tape to secure the tubing to a post so the other funnel is about two feet from the ground. Children can talk back and forth to each other through the funnels.

Fence Painting

Materials
- [ ] sheet of Plexiglas
- [ ] drill, wire
- [ ] tempera paints, brushes

Directions Drill holes in the top of the Plexiglas and attach it to the fence with wire. Let the children paint on the Plexiglas, then just hose it down to clean it.

Variations Hang a shower caddie on the fence to hold paints.

Let children fingerpaint with shaving cream on low windows or a Plexiglas easel.

Give children old ribbon or plastic strips to weave through chain-link fences.

Mailbox

Materials
- ☐ old mailbox
- ☐ box of tissues
- ☐ wet disposable towels
- ☐ hand sanitizer
- ☐ first aid kit

Directions Mount an old mailbox on the playground and store first aid supplies and tissues in it for emergency situations.

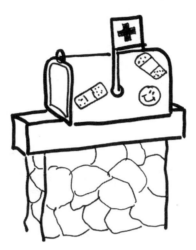

PART 2
Creating Your
Wonderful Room

Consider these three A's in designing environments for children:

Aesthetics is the love of beautiful things. For children to learn to appreciate beautiful things, they must be surrounded by the best we can give them. According to research studies, children are happier, get along better, concentrate better, and have a more positive attitude about themselves and school when they are in a beautiful environment. The aesthetics in your school can be enhanced by following these guidelines:

Focus—Children, their activities, and their art should be the focus of the room. They should provide the color.

Light—Make the classroom as light as possible, with large, open windows. Pull up blinds and shades to capitalize on natural lighting.

Neutrals—Keep the walls light and use neutral colors. Use wooden furniture, shelves, and equipment when possible.

Softness—Add pillows, soft sculpture, rugs, and window treatments to make the room look like home rather than an institution.

Nature—Bring the outdoors inside with plants, flowers, rocks, shells, and other natural objects.

Senses—A variety of textures, sounds, sights, and smells should surround children. Fresh air, flowers, evergreens, and shaving cream for fingerpainting will add pleasant sensory experiences.

Order—Provide children with a sense of order and avoid clutter. Group like objects together and organize the classroom so children can take out materials and put them away independently.

Balance and Harmony—Too many toys, posters, and objects in the room create visual overload and interfere with children's learning. Make the classroom interesting but peaceful, with a balance of pictures and materials. Rotate toys and games to maintain children's interest.

Detail—Pay attention to little details. Take the time to carefully arrange and display children's art.

Ambiance refers to the mood, character, and atmosphere in the school. Children should be immersed in harmony, warmth, and acceptance when they walk through the door. Everything about the school, from the furniture to the artwork, should say, "This is a place for children. This is a place where children come first." These principles can have a positive effect on creating the ambiance you desire in your school:

Ownership—Create a truly child-centered classroom by including children in decisions about how to set up the classroom and decorate areas. Ask them which areas they like or dislike and why. How would they make the classroom better? What would they do if they were the teacher?

Size—Furniture, sinks, door handles, and other fixtures should fit the size of the children. Adapt equipment and spaces for children with special needs.

Eye Level—Display the children's art and materials at their eye level—not at the adult level.

Privacy—Create cozy spaces and distinct areas where children can play in small groups. (Children are more likely to run around with large, open areas.)

Location—Related learning centers should be located near each other. A cozy reading corner could be near a writing center and away from the classroom door. The art center might be near the science center, with the sand and water tables in the same area.

Sound—Don't overwhelm children with noise. Keep your voice down and the children will, too. Use classical music or other peaceful music to quiet children.

Physical Development—Have areas available for gross-motor development as well as fine-motor development. Playing hopscotch on the tile floor or a beanbag toss game are just as important as learning to hold a pencil properly.

Safety and Security—Clean, safe environments will help keep children healthy and will make them feel secure.

Attitude suggests respect for individual children and their families. Children should be encouraged to make choices, laugh, play, and learn in their own unique ways. The classroom should be set up like a children's discovery museum, with many open-ended activities. Attitude about children and how they learn is reflected in the following:

DAP—Use developmentally appropriate practices and materials to enable children to explore, be independent, and feel successful.

Play—Play is what children do best and enjoy most. It is their work, and should be integrated into all areas of the curriculum.

Friends—Encourage children to interact with their friends by talking, questioning, and helping each other. Use cooperative groups to work on projects.

Meaning—Provide children with authentic learning experiences that grow out of their interests and issues important to them.

Activity—Children learn by doing! They need to move, use their senses, talk, and interact with concrete materials.

Modeling—Modeling is one of the most powerful ways children learn. Demonstrate what you want children to do, and they will imitate you.

Interaction—The more teachers interact with children in a positive, nurturing way, the more likely children are to be successful in all areas of development. Talk with children and show a genuine interest in the things they do.

Repetition—Allow children to repeat activities and experience a wide variety of materials so that skills are reinforced.

Success—It's true: nothing succeeds like success! Create an environment that is risk-free, where all children can feel worthy and competent.

Diversity—Reflect the diversity of all the people in our society with bias-free pictures, toys, books, and materials that represent different genders, ages, abilities, and cultures. Celebrate how people are alike and how they are different!

Wholeness—Learning should be connected and integrated into all areas of the curriculum. Education should also be focused on the whole child by meeting his or her physical, social, emotional, and intellectual needs.

Back It Up

The backs of exposed shelves can provide another learning area for children.

Materials
- ☐ felt and flannel board story pieces
- ☐ wipe-off boards
- ☐ glue
- ☐ mirrors

Directions

Cover the back of a shelf with felt.

Mount a wipe-off board to the back or side of furniture.

Attach a wipe-off board to a wall or shelf. (Add a small basket with markers and an eraser.)

Use mirrors on the backs of equipment.

Variations

Display children's art or photographs on the backs of shelves.

Tape large sheets of paper on the backs of shelves, and then let children decorate with crayons and markers.

Look Up! Look Down! Look All Around!

Add variety and interest to the classroom with these ideas.

Look Up!

Materials ☐ scarves, strips of fabric

Directions Loop the scarves or fabric under ceiling tile beams to create softness and diffuse light.

Variations Hang a kite, windsock, or birdhouse from the ceiling.

Tape pictures to the ceiling so children have something to look at when they nap or have quiet time.

Let the children decorate construction paper with paints or markers. They might illustrate alphabet letters, numerals, their families, friends, etc. Tape the illustrations to the ceiling.

Look Down!

Materials ☐ colorful pictures of pets, people, food
☐ clear contact paper

Directions Put the pictures on the floor and cover them with clear contact paper.

Variations Put children's photographs or artwork on the floor and cover them with the contact paper.

Use colored tape on the floor to make lines, shapes, or letters on which the children can walk.

Attach footprints to the floor to show children where to line up.

STEP IT UP

Put shapes, mathematical symbols, and words on the floor to provide a challenge to children. Have children name the shapes, write number sentences using the mathematical symbols, and write sentences using the words.

Look All Around!

Materials ☐ colored cellophane, plastic wrap, or acetate; tape

Directions Tape sheets of transparent colors to windows at the children's eye level so they can look through them out the window. (Tape just the top edge so children can lift the colored sheets.)

Variations Let children paint windows with tempera or other washable paint.

Make portholes through which the children can look. Cover the bottom portion of the window with black paper, and then cut out circles and other shapes.

Invisible Walls and Wall Hangings

Here are some unique ideas to break down large areas and create cozy spaces. These hangings can also be used on walls to add softness and texture.

Handprint Sheets*

Materials
☐ old sheets (white works best)
☐ paint
☐ pie pans

Directions
Pour the paint into the pie pans. Let children dip their hands in the paint, and then apply them on the sheet. Hang it from the ceiling as a divider.

Variations
Children can also decorate sheets with fabric crayons or markers. Older children could sew buttons, ribbons, lace, or felt shapes on old sheets to make wall hangings.

Fabric and Scarves*

Materials
☐ strips of bright-colored fabric or scarves

Directions
Hang fabric or scarves from the ceiling to add softness and to separate areas.

* To hang, insert jumbo paper clips in the top of the hanging, and then tuck the ends of the paper clips under the ceiling tile beams.

Curtain*

Materials ☐ clear shower curtain with a colorful design

Directions Create light-filled spaces by hanging the shower curtain between different areas of the classroom.

Variation Let children draw their own designs with permanent markers on a transparent shower curtain liner.

Six-Pack Plastic Rings*

Materials ☐ plastic rings from six-pack drink cans
☐ yarn, twist ties, or pipe cleaners

Directions Tie the six-pack sections together with yarn, twist ties, or pipe cleaners. Hang them from a wall or ceiling and attach children's work with clothespins.

Variation Give children different colors of yarn or ribbon to weave through the rings.

* To hang, insert jumbo paper clips in the top of the hanging, and then tuck the ends of the paper clips under the ceiling tile beams.

Bead Rooms

Materials
☐ long pieces of yarn that extend from the ceiling nearly to the floor
☐ large stringing beads with holes large enough to string on yarn
☐ several drinking straws of different colors

Directions Give each child a piece of yarn with a knot tied in one end, 10–20 large beads, and several straws. Have children string the beads on the yarn, using the straws between the beads. Hang the strings of beads next to each other from the ceiling to form a "doorway" between one area of the classroom and another.

Netting

Materials
☐ net fabric
☐ paper clips

Directions Hang the net from the ceiling with paper clips to create a special space. Attach natural objects (leaves, vines, flowers) to the net, or decorate with holiday or seasonal art.

Variation Hang a fishnet from the ceiling and attach children's work with clothespins.

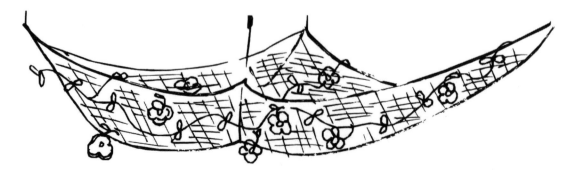

Window Treatments

Windows can be a great location to display children's work and brighten up a room.

Sun Catchers

Materials
- ☐ fishing line
- ☐ colorful opaque beads for stringing
- ☐ dowel rods cut in 6" lengths
- ☐ tape

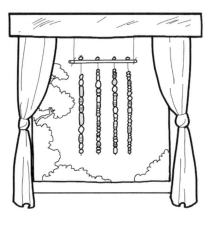

Directions Cut the fishing line into 6" pieces, and tie a knot in one end of each piece. Give each child four pieces of fishing line, and have children string beads on the lines. Tie each child's beads onto a dowel rod. Tie extra fishing line to the top of the dowel rod to use as a hanger. Use clear tape to attach the sun catchers to a window.

Weather Artists

Materials
- ☐ white butcher paper
- ☐ markers
- ☐ painting/drawing easel

Directions Set up an easel with butcher paper on it near a window so children can see outside as they draw. Have children look out the window to see what the weather is like. Ask children to draw the weather on the butcher paper. You can hang children's drawings on the window for the rest of the day.

Colorful Words

Materials
- ☐ tissue paper squares in a variety of colors
- ☐ 11" × 17" black construction paper
- ☐ pencils
- ☐ scissors
- ☐ block letters that can be traced
- ☐ tape
- ☐ string

Directions Choose some new vocabulary or spelling words that children are learning. Have each child use the block letters to form one word and trace the word on the black construction paper. Have children cut out *only* the letters in the word, without cutting the construction paper into pieces. Then have children tape tissue paper behind each empty space where the letters were on the construction paper. When children turn the construction paper over, they should see the word in multiple colors. Hang the words on the window so the sun can shine through the new words.

Borders

Borders tend to tie a room together. Adapt colors, shapes, and fabrics to blend in with your room.

Materials
- ☐ heavy fabric, wallpaper, or children's art
- ☐ scissors
- ☐ border pattern
- ☐ tape or sticky-tack

Directions   Measure the walls in the room. Select a fabric, wallpaper, or art project that you like. Use the pattern below to cut out enough pieces to go around the room. Use sticky-tack or tape to hang it near the ceiling.

Variations   Bulletin board borders or contact paper can be used in a similar manner. Let children color or paint on adding machine rolls and use them for borders.

HINT   Small checks, stripes, solids, polka dots, plaids, and tiny prints work well. Avoid large, complicated designs.

STEP IT UP   Give older children strips of paper to create tessellations that can be used as classroom borders. A tessellation is a pattern that repeats, completely fills the space, and doesn't have any gaps or overlaps. You can have children draw their tessellations freehand or trace pattern blocks. You might wish to have students use a computer drawing program to create their tessellations and print them out.

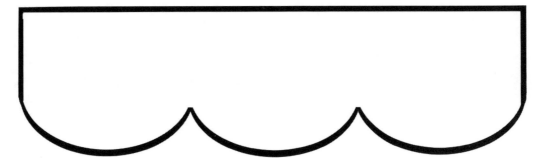

 **Reproducible Page**

Dive-In Pool

This pool will give children a defined place to play and will create a cozy space in the classroom.

Materials
- ☐ plastic swimming pool
- ☐ pillows, quilt
- ☐ books, magazines

Directions Place the pool in a quiet area of the room. Fill the pool with pillows, a quilt, books, and magazines. Let several children at a time "dive in" and read.

Variations Add writing materials, word search or crossword puzzle games, pattern blocks, play dough, and other manipulatives to the pool.

Take the pool out onto the playground and make a quiet area where children can read and relax.

Box It

Boxes invite children to use their imaginations, and they create wonderful props and little spaces for play.

Materials
- ☐ large corrugated cardboard boxes (appliance boxes work well)
- ☐ utility knife*
- ☐ paints, markers, crayons

Directions   Ask children to suggest things they could make out of the boxes. Cut out doors and windows with a utility knife, and then let children decorate the boxes with markers, crayons, paints, and their imaginations.

Variations   Divide the class into small groups; give each group a large box, and let children design their own houses. They can paint the outside, wallpaper the inside, and add other details.

Ask children to use the boxes to create the setting of a story the class has read recently.

Have children use the boxes to create different types of animal homes, such as a nest, a burrow, or a cave.

* Keep knife out of children's reach.

Bag It

Create a center full of bags and purses that children can fill and carry around.

Materials
- ☐ purses
- ☐ billfolds
- ☐ cloth bags
- ☐ change purse
- ☐ briefcase
- ☐ keys
- ☐ small suitcase
- ☐ basket
- ☐ paper bags with handles
- ☐ paper and pencils
- ☐ toys and goodies (vary for the age of the children)

Directions Place all the bags on a shelf or hang them on a low hat rack. Put keys, billfolds, and small items in a basket. Children can fill the bags with different objects and carry them around.

Variations Use knobs from kitchen cabinets on the front of a shelf to hang bags.

If you have tile walls, attach plastic hooks with adhesive backs to hang purses or other bags.

Take bags and baskets onto the playground so children can collect leaves and other natural objects.

Ask parents to donate old purses, bags, and briefcases.

HINT Cut the straps off the bags or tie them in knots if they are too long for little ones.

Help Yourself Pockets

A shoe bag can be a handy way to display materials and create learning centers. It can be hung from the back of a shelf, on a door, on a wall, or even on a playground fence.

Materials
- ☐ clear plastic shoe bags
- ☐ art materials
- ☐ writing materials
- ☐ math materials
- ☐ science materials
- ☐ natural objects
- ☐ toys
- ☐ music materials

Art Pockets Use shoe pockets to hold art materials such as scissors, glue, crayons, markers, tape, yarn, paper scraps, collage materials, and recycled objects. Hang the bag near a table so children can help themselves while creating pictures and sculptures. For outdoor art, carry the shoe bag out onto the playground and hang it on a fence near a picnic table.

Writer's Nook Fill shoe pockets with pens, pencils, sticky notes, envelopes, different kinds of paper, stamps, story starter ideas, and word lists.

Science Surprise Place a magnifying glass, magnet, prism, spring scale, field guide, bones, shells, leaves, and other interesting objects in the pockets.

Toy Bag Put cars, trucks, dolls, rattles, small balls, and other age-appropriate toys in the bag.

Math Pockets Put a calculator, paper, pencils, flash cards, pattern blocks, rulers, 3-D shapes, and other math items in the shoe pockets.

Music, Music Display rhythm sticks, bells, shakers, and other instruments in pockets.

HINT Shoe bags can be cut in half to create two centers.

Texture Board

Children will enjoy exploring these different textures, and they'll be challenged to identify them with their eyes closed.

Materials
- ☐ large poster board
- ☐ glue
- ☐ various textures such as cotton, rice, gravel, feathers, corrugated cardboard, contact paper (sticky side), satin, burlap, bubble wrap, aluminum foil, yarn, sandpaper, macaroni, and confetti

Directions
Glue small samples of the textures onto the poster board. Hang the poster board on the back of a shelf or door. Have children touch the different objects and describe how the objects feel.

Variations
Ask children to close their eyes and identify the different textures.

Glue textures to index cards. (Make two of each texture.) Let children spread them out and try to match them up with their eyes closed.

Take texture cards out onto the playground and see if children can find similar textures in nature.

STEP IT UP
Have children write sentences or paragraphs to describe the different textures they feel. Encourage children to use adjectives to accurately describe the textures.

A Touch of Nature

Nature has a calming effect, so bring the outside inside with these ideas.

Beauty Display plants and flowers in the classroom. Grow seeds and cuttings.

Animals Display pictures of animals and insects that are common to your area. If allergies are not an issue, have local experts bring animals to your school for assemblies.

Investigation Place leaves, seeds, grass, flowers, dirt, and other natural objects in a water table for exploration.

Art Paint with sticks, pine needles, and flowers. Let children glue natural objects onto cardboard and paper plates to create a collage.

Math Give children leaves, flowers, and rocks to sort, count, add, and make patterns with.

STEP IT UP To help children develop their problem-solving skills, write word problems for children to solve using objects found in nature. For example: "There are three children. Each child finds five rocks. How many rocks do they find in all?" (15)

Science Rotate natural objects in the science area. Encourage children to bring interesting things they find at home to add to the collection.

Concept Basket Take a basket outside and challenge children to find all the green things they can on the playground. Upon returning to the classroom, have children spread them out and sort, count, etc. (Find objects that have different shapes, objects that are soft, objects that are yellow, etc.)

Bird Watching

Children of all ages will get into bird watching with this feeder outside your classroom window.

Materials
- ☐ clear vegetable oil bottle
- ☐ scissors, hole punch
- ☐ wooden stick
- ☐ birdseed
- ☐ field guide to birds
- ☐ two cardboard rollers
- ☐ string, tape, pipe cleaner

Directions Make a bird feeder from the vegetable oil bottle by cutting windows in the sides. Insert a stick in the bottom for a perch, fill the bottle with birdseed, and tie it onto a tree near a classroom window with the pipe cleaner. Make binoculars from the cardboard rollers. Place the binoculars and bird identification book near a window where children can see the feeder. Children can then try to identify the birds they see at the feeder in the book.

Variations Ask children to do a weather watch and draw what the weather is like outside the window.

Give children real binoculars. Encourage them to be world watchers and look for all the animals, plants, people, or other objects they can see outside the window.

Have children write descriptive paragraphs to tell about the things they see outside the window. Encourage children to share their paragraphs with the class.

Play Trays

Lunchroom trays give children a defined area in which to work. Furthermore, they get children involved with materials that are often forgotten on shelves.

Materials
- ☐ lunchroom trays (available at restaurant supply stores)
- ☐ manipulative toys
- ☐ sensory materials

Directions Place two to four trays on a table with materials similar to the ones below:

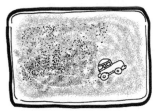

cutting—scrap paper and scissors

molding—play dough, cookie cutters, scissors, plastic pizza cutter, etc.

punching—hole punch and tickets or scrap paper

writing—blank books, markers, crayons, pens, pencils

drawing—small whiteboard, dry-erase markers, eraser

sand—sand, small animals, cars, trucks (Older children can practice writing their names, letters, numerals, or spelling words in the sand.)

landforms—make pictures of common landforms, such as a cove, island, or peninsula, and let children reproduce them in a tray with sand

textures—beans and rice, cornmeal, oatmeal, wet noodles, and other textures are fun to explore in trays

painting—fingerpaint with shaving cream or hand lotion, or fingerpaint in trays

puzzles—puzzles and pieces will stay together in trays

beads and sewing cards—display lacing cards, stringing beads, pegboards, and other small toys

stencils—stencils, templates, colored pencils, and paper

HINT By using a small table with two trays facing each other, you can encourage communication and cooperation.

Puppet Theater

Puppets are a magical way for children to express their thoughts, feelings, and imaginations. Puppets also encourage social skills, problem solving, and language development among children. This puppet theater will provide children with a special way to act out stories, songs, rhymes, and real-life situations.

Materials
- ☐ large appliance box
- ☐ utility knife*
- ☐ fabric
- ☐ glue
- ☐ markers or paints

Directions   Cut a hole in one side of the box to be the stage of the puppet theater. (An adult will need to do this.) Cut a door in the back of the box so children can get into it. Glue a fabric ruffle to the top of the stage. Let children decorate the box with markers or paints.

Variations   Use a tension curtain rod and old curtain across a door frame to create a puppet theater.

Let children make tickets for their puppet shows and invite other classes to their performances.

Tie in puppet productions with literature, themes, songs, or celebrations.

* Keep knife out of children's reach.

Puppets, Puppets, Puppets!

Here are some delightful puppets children will enjoy creating and using in the puppet theater.

Sock Puppets   Let children decorate old socks with markers, buttons, yarn, wiggly eyes, and other art supplies to create puppets they can wear on their hands.

Stick Puppets   Have children cut animals or characters out of construction paper and glue the cutouts to craft sticks.

People Puppets   Cut pictures of people out of magazines or catalogs and staple them to straws.

Hanger Puppets   Stretch a coat hanger into a diamond shape. Pull a leg from an old pair of pantyhose over the hanger and knot it at the bottom. Decorate the puppet with paper scraps, felt, wiggly eyes, buttons, yarn hair, etc.

Envelope Puppets   Recycle used envelopes by cutting them in half. Decorate each one with markers or crayons and insert your fingers in the opening.

Spoon Puppets   Use wooden ice cream spoons to make puppets by drawing on them with fine tip markers.

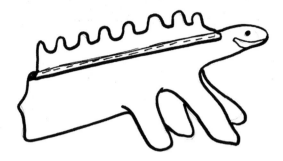

Dinosaur Puppets Cut a 7" slit up the back of a rubber glove. Make spikes for the dinosaur by cutting zigzags in a 7" × 3" piece of felt. Staple the felt in the slit in the glove; draw a face with markers on the middle finger as shown above.

Sack Puppets Decorate lunch sacks with construction paper scraps, crayons, markers, and collage materials to create puppets.

Paper Plates Staple two paper plates together ¾ of the way around. Draw on the plates with markers or crayons; insert your hand into the opening.

Glove Puppets Cut the fingers off old gloves; decorate them with markers, felt scraps, or wiggly eyes to make worms, insects, or little people.

Cardboard Rollers Decorate toilet paper rolls with markers, paints, or construction paper to make puppets.

Finger Puppets Cut out small characters from paper and glue them to 2½" strips. Wrap the strips into circles, tape them, and wear them around your fingers.

Busy Boxes

Busy boxes are a convenient way to store self-contained activities that can be used by individual children or small groups of children. They're perfect for entertaining children who arrive early or those who finish other activities early. You can also use them to enhance learning centers by rotating props in the block area, adding collage materials in the art center, or adding props in the dramatic play area.

Busy boxes can be made from shoe boxes, detergent boxes with handles, or plastic tubs. Cover the cardboard boxes with contact paper or spray-paint to make them more attractive. Also, label the boxes with words and picture cues.

Mail Box — Fill with junk mail, paper, envelopes, pens, and pencils.

Punch and Snip — Add a hole punch, scissors, and scrap paper.

Math Kit — Put in manipulatives to sort and count, a ruler, a minute timer, play money, a calculator, paper, and pencils.

Sewing Box — Add beads, buttons, straws, and pasta (with holes) to string on yarn, shoelaces, ribbon, or string. Burlap, plastic needles, yarn, and sewing cards can also be used.

Animal Safari — Put in zoo animals, arctic animals, farm animals, dinosaurs, and berry baskets for cages.

Let's Go — Small cars, trucks, planes, boats, and road signs will keep children zooming around.

Grab Bag Art — Fill with paper scraps, recycled junk, collage materials, crayons, glue, scissors, etc.

Writer's Kit — Add blank books, envelopes, sticky notes, stamps, notepads, pencils, pens, and markers.

Game Time — A deck of cards, concentration cards, flash cards, dice, or dominoes can be stored in a box.

Play Dough Factory Give children cookie cutters, a plastic pizza cutter, scissors, textured objects, toy dishes, plastic wrap, and a plastic knife to use with the dough.

Puppet Pals Fill a box with finger puppets, stick puppets, or hand puppets.

Dress Me Put in an old shoe and shoelace, zipper, buttons, Velcro, snaps (cut-off old garments), and buckles (cut 10" from old belts and punch holes).

My Puppy Children will have fun playing with a stuffed dog, grooming brush, leash, plastic bowl, empty food container, plastic dog biscuits, dog toys, etc.

Jewelry Box Add costume jewelry, old watches, scarves, a mirror, hair bows, hair clips, and gloves.

Concept Boxes Collect objects beginning with a certain sound, objects of a like color, or objects of a like shape.

Odds and Ends Keys, wind-up toys, music boxes, a kaleidoscope, a magnifying glass, and other objects will interest children.

Story Box Put in a book and puppets or toys for acting out the story.

Baby Box Fill a box with a baby doll or stuffed animal, clothes, a blanket, a bottle, and other baby items.

Making Music Add musical instruments and other things that can be used to make noise.

Sports Bag Tennis balls, sponge balls, beach balls, a jump rope, bean bags, a visor, and pom poms can be used in a sports bag.

Picture Box Fill a box with pictures from magazines, calendars, toy catalogs, photographs of the children, or family photos.

A Quiet Place

There will be times when children need to be alone to think, relax, release emotions, or gain self-control. The "Quiet Place" provides children with an area where they can have privacy and peace.

Materials
- ☐ large box
- ☐ pillows and carpet squares
- ☐ beanbag chair
- ☐ stuffed animal
- ☐ mirror
- ☐ scarf or fabric
- ☐ classical music

Directions Decorate a large appliance box to look like a doghouse or clubhouse. Put carpet squares on the floor and add pillows or books.

Variations Pull a shelf away from a wall to make a cozy corner. Add a beanbag chair, a pillow, a stuffed animal, and a mirror.

Drape a large scarf or piece of fabric between two shelves to create a "dream center." Add pictures of peaceful places and pillows. Play soft music.

Portfolio Place

Portfolios provide ongoing assessment and are a way to document how children are developing and how they use skills. Portfolios show what children can do, and give a more inclusive view of different areas of growth.

Materials
- ☐ file folders
- ☐ photographs of children
- ☐ glue
- ☐ markers, crayons
- ☐ plastic crate

Directions   To make portfolios, glue each child's picture to the top of a file folder. Let children decorate the outside of their portfolios with markers or crayons. Store the portfolios in a plastic crate in a convenient place in the classroom and label it "Portfolio Place." Encourage children to file pictures or stories they write in their portfolios. Other items that can be included in portfolios are:

- ☐ self-portraits
- ☐ art projects
- ☐ writing samples (scribbles, name, journal)
- ☐ work samples (math, group projects, motor activities)
- ☐ anecdotal records (funny sayings, special moments)
- ☐ photographs
- ☐ dictated stories
- ☐ teacher observations
- ☐ CDs of children talking or reading
- ☐ summary of parent conferences

HINT   Date all items in portfolios, and then use them to communicate with parents at conference time.

Family Culture Box

These boxes will celebrate the families in your classroom, while providing children with a meaningful multicultural activity.

Materials
- ☐ boxes with lids
- ☐ postcards, books, clothes, cooking items (empty boxes), games, toys, travel brochures, ethnic restaurant menus, CDs, DVDs, artwork, etc.

Directions Ask parents and children to donate some of the above objects or other items that reflect their culture. (Explain that the children will be playing with these things, so they should not include anything valuable.) Put each child's objects in a box with the child's name and the culture represented by the objects. Let individual children share their culture boxes with classmates. Leave the boxes open for free exploration, or put various objects in centers around the room. For example, cooking utensils and food boxes could be placed in the dramatic play area, books in the library, or CDs or DVDs in the computer center.

Variations Compare the items in different culture boxes. How are they alike? How are they different?

Ask parents to read a book to the class in their native language. (They could also make a CD.)

Ask parents to send in a picture of a family celebration. Put the pictures in a scrapbook for children to look at, or make a computer slideshow using the pictures.

Play with Me

(Home/School Learning Tasks)

This is an exciting way to involve parents in extending their children's learning at home with fun projects and quality time.

Materials
- ☐ library pockets or envelopes cut in half
- ☐ poster board
- ☐ markers, glue
- ☐ 3" x 5" index cards

Directions Write each child's name on a library pocket or envelope. Print "Play with Me" on the poster board, and then glue the pockets onto the poster board as shown. Write a different activity children can do at home with their parents on each index card. (Use the suggestions on the following page, or make up your own to reflect your children's abilities and interests and your curriculum.) Send a note home to parents about the learning tasks that their child will bring home each week. Remind parents to have fun with their child as they do the activity, and to return the card by the end of the week. Place a different card in each child's pocket at the beginning of each week, and follow up with parents about how they are enjoying the activities.

Variations Number the activities and keep a graph to help with record keeping.

Make a vacation fun pack for families with the activities on the following page. Make copies of the activities, and then cut them up and put the strips in a can or box that the children have decorated. Tell children that they can pick something special to do from the can each day they are on vacation.

Home/School Activities

1. Take a walk together.
2. Say your phone number and address.
3. Help fold the laundry.
4. Count the doors in your home.
5. Look for something beautiful outside.
6. Can you find ten things in your home that are red?
7. Read a book together.
8. Put on some music and make up a dance.
9. Find a picture in a magazine and write a story or draw a picture about it.
10. Draw a healthy breakfast on a paper plate.
11. Can you hop, skip, gallop, and jump?
12. Say some nursery rhymes.
13. Practice what you would do if there were a fire at your home.
14. Find eight objects that are smaller than your thumb.
15. Teach a song to your family.
16. Think of words that rhyme with "man," "cat," "like," "big," "hot," and "bee."
17. Write a haiku about something in nature near your home.
18. Go on a shape hunt around your home; find squares, triangles, and circles.
19. Play a game like "Hide and Go Seek" or "I Spy."
20. Name the months in the year.
21. Draw a picture for someone you love.
22. Go outside at night. What can you see in the sky? What sounds do you hear?
23. If you had three wishes, what would you wish for?
24. Find something that starts with b, m, s, f, l, r, and h.
25. Plan a party or special outing for your family.
26. Give a back rub to someone in your family.
27. Say "Please" and "Thank you" all day.
28. How many canned foods do you have in your kitchen?
29. Make a paper sack puppet.
30. Make up some jokes or funny riddles.

 **Reproducible Page**

Top Ten Storage Tips

Teachers are packrats by nature, but these storage tips will eliminate clutter and improve organization.

1. Toss it in the trash. If you don't use it anymore, get rid of it!

2. Purchase clear plastic storage containers. Try to select boxes that you can stack on top of each other. Label the contents on the end of each box. (If you use cardboard boxes instead, spray-paint or cover them with contact paper so they all look alike.)

3. Hide messy shelves and cabinets with curtains, murals, or posters. Use tablecloths to hide objects stored under a table, such as in the science center.

4. Group like objects together in a logical place where they are used. File materials by month, teaching themes, content areas, etc.

5. Rotate toys, books, and materials. When children are no longer interested in something, put it away and get out something new.

6. Put bulletin boards in garbage bags, and then hang them on skirt hangers in a closet. (Store language experience charts and posters in the same way or use a garment bag.)

7. Pizza boxes, plastic tubs, plastic bags, plastic crates, clear food containers, detergent boxes, and shoe boxes can all be used for storing art supplies and manipulatives. Label each with the appropriate word and picture.

8. Put toys and art supplies on low shelves where children can reach them. Take the time to teach children how to care for materials and clean up after themselves. (Teacher materials should be kept on high shelves or in closets.)

9. Put odds and ends and bits and pieces that you don't know what to do with on the art table for children to use in collages and sculptures.

10. Do a major clean-up at the end of each month. After several weeks of looking at the same bulletin board or display, children generally lose interest in it.

 **Reproducible Page**

Classroom Rating Scale

Use this classroom rating scale to help you determine your strengths and weaknesses. Make goals for improvement based on the areas indicated below.

	Almost Always	To Some Extent	Needs Improvement
Children are generally happy and excited about coming into your classroom.			
Children are actively engaged in activities and rarely wander around.			
Children interact cooperatively with each other and seldom argue.			
Most of the pictures and displays in the classroom are made by the children.			
Language experience stories and other examples of print are utilized.			
The classroom reflects cultural diversity with books, posters, toys, and other bias-free materials.			
Family photographs are displayed.			
There are places where children can be alone.			
Soft elements (e.g., rugs, pillows) are included in the classroom.			
Learning centers and shelves are labeled.			
Children can make choices about where they want to play.			
There are opportunities for large group, small group, and independent learning.			
There is a balance of active and quiet times.			
Children play outside daily.			
Children are given large blocks of time (45 minutes to an hour) to engage in learning centers.			

 **Reproducible Page**

	Almost Always	To Some Extent	Needs Improvement
Children can get out and put away materials independently.			
There are at least four choices of activities in each learning center.			
Learning center activities are related to current units of study.			
Learning center activities reflect options for independent, partner, and small group work.			
The classroom is neat and free of clutter.			
Materials are rotated in the different learning centers to maintain interest.			
Dramatic play and other areas are integrated with units of study.			
Plants and natural objects are used in the classroom.			
There is an open art area so children can create on their own.			
Different learning styles and abilities are provided for.			
There is enough space for children to move around and work freely.			
Children can work independently with little adult supervision.			
Classroom expectations are clear and simple so children understand them.			

 **Reproducible Page**

PART 3
Creating a Literate Environment

Children should be immersed in language so they can begin to appreciate its beauty and importance at an early age.

This section will show you how to use labels, signs, and language experience charts in your classroom in meaningful ways. Suggestions for making books, a creative alphabet, and rebus activity cards will also be presented.

Signs

Signs can be used to encourage reading and writing skills, to demonstrate how functional language is, and to remind children of appropriate behavior.

Put a reminder on the back of the bathroom door.

Use a sign to show where riding toys should be parked.

Use signs on the classroom door to show where you are.

Create bilingual signs.

 **STEP IT UP** Have children create bilingual signs for different areas of the classroom, using different languages. Children may label the art center in English, Spanish, French, and Chinese, for example.

Charts and Posters

Use charts and posters daily to reinforce the usefulness of reading and writing.

Sign In   Make an attendance poster that has a pocket for each child with her name on it. Let each child draw her face on a circle and attach it to a popsicle stick. As children come into the classroom each day, have each child select her stick from a basket, then place it in a pocket with her name on it. (Real photos of the children's faces can also be used.)

Job Chart   Write jobs on a poster, then write children's names on cutouts of hands. Attach Velcro™ to the backs of the hand cutouts and to the poster so that each child can put his name by the job he would like to do.

Daily Schedule   Write your daily schedule on a poster. (Use a clothespin to mark your progress through the schedule as you complete different activities.)

Song Chart   Let children tell you their favorite songs and write them on a poster. Add a picture clue for each song. When you need a song, ask a child to choose one from the chart.

Songs and Poems   Write words to songs, poems, or finger plays on charts. Point to the words as children say or sing them.

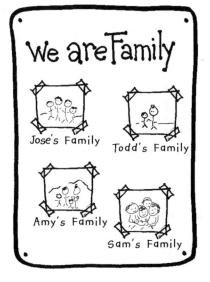

Family Photos   Display photos of children's families.

Grandparents   Ask children to bring in pictures of their grandparents. Hang them on a poster and label.

*Language experience charts reinforce the following concept:
"What I say can be written down, and what is written down
I can read."*

Happiness Is...

Tasha - Spending the night with Granny.

Josh- Riding my bike.

Sami- Getting my new bird Tweetie.

Beth- My birthday, party!

Complete a Sentence   Ask children to complete an open-ended sentence.

Field Trip   Follow up a field trip with a story about it.

The Pumpkin Patch

We went to Farmer Joe's Pumpkin Patch.

We rode a big yellow Bus.

We had a picnic.

Message Board

Don't forget!

Messages   Use a message board with sticky notes as a reminder to you and the children.

Unit of Study   Relate language experience charts to a unit of study.

When I Grow Up

Sadik - I might be a fire fighter.

Maria - I want to be a doctor.

Fritz - I'm going to be a baseball player.

Cutouts   Write children's individual responses to questions on cutouts, then tape them onto a door.

Class Rules   Let children help formulate classroom rules. Refer to the rules when there is a conflict.

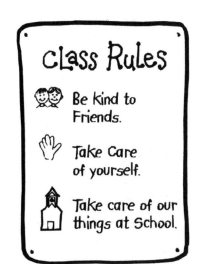

Today's Special   Write a message to the children each morning welcoming them. Include the special activities you will do that day.

Star Student   Highlight unique qualities of a different child each week. Include her picture, likes, dislikes, favorite books, pets, etc.

Daily News   At the end of the school day, have the children recall the events of the day in sequence. Write down what they liked best or what they learned.

Homework   Write down a homework assignment or extension activity children can do each evening. Have the children read over it with you before they leave each day.

Rebus Activity Charts

Rebus cards encourage children to "read pictures," follow directions, and work independently.

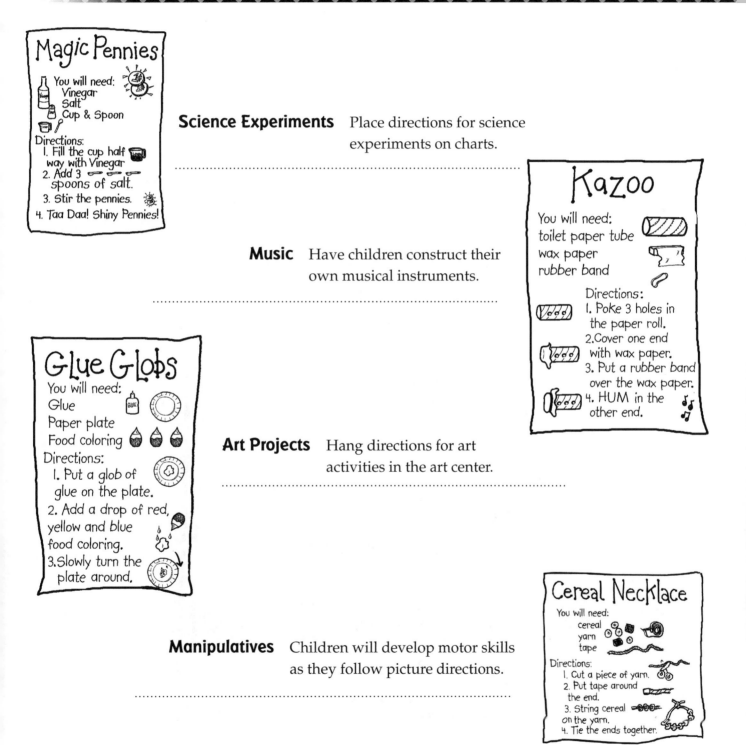

Magic Pennies

You will need:
Vinegar
Salt
Cup & Spoon

Directions:
1. Fill the cup half way with Vinegar
2. Add 3 spoons of salt.
3. Stir the pennies.
4. Taa Daa! Shiny Pennies!

Science Experiments   Place directions for science experiments on charts.

Music   Have children construct their own musical instruments.

Kazoo

You will need:
toilet paper tube
wax paper
rubber band

Directions:
1. Poke 3 holes in the paper roll.
2. Cover one end with wax paper.
3. Put a rubber band over the wax paper.
4. HUM in the other end.

Glue Globs

You will need:
Glue
Paper plate
Food coloring

Directions:
1. Put a glob of glue on the plate.
2. Add a drop of red, yellow and blue food coloring.
3. Slowly turn the plate around.

Art Projects   Hang directions for art activities in the art center.

Cereal Necklace

You will need:
cereal
yarn
tape

Directions:
1. Cut a piece of yarn.
2. Put tape around the end.
3. String cereal on the yarn.
4. Tie the ends together.

Manipulatives   Children will develop motor skills as they follow picture directions.

Cook's Nook

Children will enjoy preparing their own snacks with rebus recipe cards. Reading, math, and self-help skills are all reinforced as children cook.

Materials
☐ large chart tablet, markers
☐ cooking utensils
☐ food

Directions
Prepare recipe and snack charts similar to the ones below and on the next page. Carefully explain the directions, serving sizes, clean-up procedures, safely precautions, etc. Allow children to work independently or in small groups as they cook their snacks. (Younger ones will need adult help.)

Spider Snack

You will need:
  1 round cracker
  6 raisins
  8 pretzel sticks
  peanut butter

Directions:
  1. Wash your hands.
  2. Spread peanut butter on the cracker.
  3. Make a face with the raisins.
  4. Add 8 pretzels for legs
  5. Clean up!

Yogurt Parfait

You will need:
1 plastic cup
Chopped strawberries,
blueberries, bananas
Granola
Spoon

Directions:
1. Wash your hands.
2. Put some yogurt in the cup.
3. Put some chopped fruit and granola in the cup.
4. Put more yogurt in the cup.
5. Put more chopped fruit and granola in the cup.
6. Clean up!

Letters, Letters, Letters

Famous People Write letters or emails to the President, Governor, movie stars, etc. (You can get their addresses at the library or on the Internet.) Frame the letters or emails you receive from famous people.

Thank You's Write thank-you notes after field trips or to thank guest speakers. School helpers and parent volunteers will also appreciate notes of thanks.

Teacher Mailbox Make a mailbox from a cereal box and encourage the children to write you letters.

Student Mailboxes Make a mailbox for each child from clasp envelopes and staple them onto a bulletin board or tape them to children's cubbies.

Junk Mail Give children junk mail to play with. (Most parents will be glad to send in their junk mail, too.)

Story Box

Stories will come alive for children as they retell them with a story box. This is a great way to extend literature and encourage language development.

Materials
- ☐ school box, cigar box, or other box with a lid attached
- ☐ felt, felt scraps
- ☐ scissors, glue
- ☐ paper, markers
- ☐ favorite books or folk tales

Directions Cut felt to fit on the inside lid of the box and glue it in place. Using felt scraps, cut out the main characters and props from one of the books. Place the book and felt characters in the box, then decorate the outside of the box with a picture and the book title. Read the book to the class and demonstrate how to use the figures inside to retell the story. Place the story box in the library so children can use it with friends.

Variations After children have practiced retelling the story, let them take home the story box and share it with their families.

Invite parents in for a workshop and have them make story boxes for the classroom.

STEP IT UP Have children choose a book they have read and have them make a story box for that book. Invite children to share their story boxes with the class.

Write Ideas

Official Report   Take a spiral ring notebook and write "official report" on it. When a child starts to tattle or complain, hand him the book and tell him to "write it down."

Newspaper Report   When children go on a field trip, assign one child to be the reporter and to write down what the children do and see.

Turns List   Keep a clipboard with paper and pencils by favorite classroom activities. Children can sign their names to indicate they are waiting for a turn. (You can also use a "turns list" on the playground for riding toys, swings, etc.)

Graphs   Integrate language and math skills with graphs.

Sign In   Place name cards by a large tablet of chart paper. Write the day and date on the top sheet before children come to school. Each day when children come to school they can find their card and write their name on the paper. Tear off the used sheet after school each day.

Writing Center   Keep name cards in the writing center so children can use their friends' names to write stories, notes, etc.

Write the Room   Give each child a clipboard with paper on it. Have children walk around the room and write down the things they see. Have children write the words in sentences.

Lifetime Words   Explain that high frequency words are "lifetime words." Once you learn them and store them in your brain, they will belong to you for the rest of your lifetime! Collect empty mint tins and let children "save" lifetime words in their tins. Have children write their words on small slips of paper. Children can collect lifetime words from books they read, classroom displays, road signs, stores, newspapers, magazines, online resources, etc.

Wipe-Off Boards

Writing skills will flourish when children are provi[...]
individual wipe-off boards.

Materials
- ☐ 8' × 4' sheet of wipe-off board
  (available at building supply stores)
- ☐ dry-erase markers
- ☐ permanent magic marker
- ☐ plastic crate or box

Directions   Cut the wipe-off board into twenty sections.
(They will usually do this where you purchase
the board.) Using the permanent marker, print each child's name at the top
of a board in dotted lines. Place the boards in a crate or box for children to
use independently. They can practice writing their names, draw pictures,
write words, etc.

Variations   Have each child bring in an old sock to use as an eraser.

Attach a wipe-off board to the wall of a classroom or hall for the children to
use for writing or drawing.

Use the boards for learning games. Have the children sit on the floor with
their boards in their laps. Ask them to reproduce shapes, make sets, write
numerals, etc. Older children could write spelling words, math facts, etc.

Stuff an empty cereal box with newspaper, then cover with white contact
paper. Children can write on the white contact paper with water soluble
markers, then erase with a wet towel.

HINT   Use only dry-erase markers for anything you want to be able to erase from
wipe-off boards.

abels

Before children read words, they read pictures. Picture and word labels reinforce reading concepts and enable children to be independent and clean up after themselves.

Materials
- ☐ school supply catalogs
- ☐ poster board or construction paper
- ☐ glue, scissors
- ☐ markers

Directions Make a list of different toys, supplies, and materials in your classroom. Cut pictures of those objects from school catalogs. Glue the pictures to small pieces of poster board or construction paper and print the words beside the pictures. Tape these labels to shelves, cabinets, boxes, and other objects.

Variations Attach labels to shelves with clear contact paper.

Use pictures from the boxes toys come in to make labels.

Let children draw their own pictures of toys and supplies to use on the labels.

Trace around objects on black paper and use the silhouettes to label shelves.

Create labels for learning centers that include pictures, a list of skills children develop from playing in the center, and the number of friends who may play there.

Letter and Number Land

This is a meaningful, hands-on way to introduce children to letters and numerals.

Materials
- ☐ poster board cut in 8" × 10" rectangles
- ☐ markers
- ☐ glue gun
- ☐ small classroom objects and toys for each letter of the alphabet

Directions Print a letter of the alphabet in the upper left corner of each card. Glue an object that begins with the sound of that letter on the card with the glue gun. (Involve the children in finding these objects in the classroom. For example, you could use a plastic apple for A, a block for B, a crayon for C, a toy dog for D, an eraser for E, a feather for F, etc.) Let the children write the name of each object on the bottom of the card as shown. Hang the letters up around the classroom at the children's eye level.

Variations Use children's names and photographs to make alphabet cards. (Take pictures of other people or objects in the school for letters for which you don't have children's names.)

Make an alphabet of environmental print by gluing labels, logos, and other familiar words to poster board.

Purchase inexpensive party favors to use in making number cards. Write the numeral on the card, then glue on that set of objects. Let the children write the words.

HINT Put a border around the outside of each card with a magic marker.

lk-About Story

All children will be motivated to read the walk-about story.

Materials
- ☐ butcher paper
- ☐ markers, crayons, or paints
- ☐ clear packaging tape

Directions

Roll out a long sheet of paper.

Mark off 2' sections on the paper.

Let each child draw his picture and write his name in one of the sections. Write the following chant in each section:

> (First name), (name) who do you see?
> I see (second child's name) looking at me.
>
> (Second name), (name) who do you see?
> I see (third child's name) looking at me.

And so forth...

Tape the paper to the floor with clear packaging tape. (You can also cover it with clear contact paper.)

Variations

Let the children write and illustrate their own original stories using a similar format.

Have the children work together to write and illustrate a story. Hang the pages in the hallway. Tape a sheet of paper to the top of each page so other students walking down the hall will be curious and will want to lift the sheets and read the story.

STEP IT UP

Have children choose a story they enjoy. Make sure each child chooses a different story. Give each child a roll of paper that is divided into ten different sections. Have children summarize the story in the sections of the paper by writing sentences and drawing pictures. Have children use their walk-about stories to retell the stories they chose to the class.

Steppin' Out a Story

Children will begin to identify important elements in a story as they physically "step it out."

Materials
☐ construction paper (different colors)
☐ markers
☐ clear contact paper

Directions Cut the construction paper into different large shapes. Write one of the following elements of a story on each of the construction paper shapes: title, character, setting, problem, and solution. Place the shapes on the floor and cover with clear contact paper. After reading a book to the children, let them stand on the different sections to identify the various parts of the story.

Variations The construction paper may also be laminated and taped to the floor.

Adapt the elements to the age and ability of the children. For older children you might include the author, illustrator, beginning, middle, and end of the story.

Homemade Books

Making books with children not only utilizes their reading and writing skills, it also encourages their creativity and problem-solving ability. Furthermore, children are motivated to read the books that they and their classmates write. These homemade books can be a great addition to your classroom library; children can also take them home and share them with their families.

Photo Album Books Purchase inexpensive photo albums with magnetic sheets. Use children's drawings, stories, or photographs to make books in the albums.

Class Books Give each child a piece of paper and ask him to write a story or draw a picture relating to a specific topic. (It might be about a unit of study, a field trip, a holiday, a school event, a favorite person, what the children want to be when they grow up, wishes, their families, feelings, etc.) Staple the children's pages inside construction paper and decorate the cover. After reading these books to the class, let different children take them home to share with their families.

Computer Books Have children type a story on the computer. Children can use drawing tools on the computer to draw their own story illustrations. They can also use clip art and photos to illustrate their stories. Have a file on the computer for all of the stories so children can read each other's stories while in the computer center.

Tag Along Books   Fold white paper (8½" × 11") inside construction paper (9" × 12") and staple along the fold. After the children have drawn pictures or written stories in these books, punch two holes along the fold. Insert a pipe cleaner in the holes and form a handle. Children can carry around their "tag along" books.

Sheet Protector Books   Put children's drawings or stories in sheet protectors. Tie together several sheet protectors with ribbon or yarn to make a book. (Newspaper articles and magazine pictures can also be put in sheet protectors to make books.)

Lunch Sack Books   Take five paper lunch sacks and fold over the bottom of each sack to make a peek-a-boo flap. Draw a picture under each flap so only part of it shows. Staple the lunch sacks together on the open end. Children can try to identify the pictures, then lift the flaps to confirm their guesses. (Magazine pictures or cutouts can also be used to make lunch sack books.)

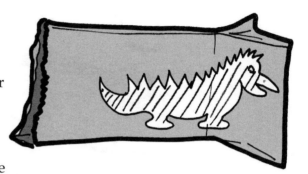

Creative Covers   Staple plain paper between pieces of wrapping paper, wallpaper, funny papers, contact paper, maps, stiff fabric, cardboard, food boxes, or other materials to make books.

Grocery Sack Big Books   Cut the fronts and backs off large paper grocery sacks to make pages. Have the children each paint or draw a picture on one of the pages, then dictate a sentence about their picture. Punch holes in the sides and tie the pages together with yarn or string. (Songs, nursery rhymes, and poems are fun to use to make these Big Books.)

Shape Books   Cut construction paper and writing paper into unusual shapes and staple to make books to motivate children to write and read. Geometric shapes, seasonal patterns, animals, or objects that relate to a unit of study can all be used.

Sentence Strip Book   Let children cut out pictures from school supply catalogs. Glue the pictures to sentence strips, then write sentences children dictate or allow them to write their own sentences to go with the pictures. Punch a hole in the left side of each sentence strip and attach them together with a book ring.

Baggie Book   Cut construction paper to fit inside plastic sandwich bags. Glue photographs of the children onto the paper and write a sentence about each of them. (Children can also draw their own pictures, or you can cut out pictures from magazines to make baggie books.) Place the pictures in the baggies and zip shut. Poke two holes in the side of each baggie, then tie them together with pipe cleaners or bread ties. (Large bags can be used to make bigger books.)

PART 4
Celebrating Children's Art

Children's art is the most refreshing, original, and charming in the world, and should be the focus of any school environment.

Rather than patterned projects and photocopies in which everyone's work looks the same, children need open-ended activities that allow them to think, experiment, problem-solve, and express themselves in unique ways. Art should be process oriented, for children enjoy the moment and are not concerned with the final product. Since art is the child's outward expression of her inner world, it can also be an emotional release and can provide a vehicle for the development of thinking processes.

▶ With art, there is no failure, but simply the joy of the experience.

▶ With art, there should be no comparison, for whatever the child creates is his or hers and should be cherished.

▶ With art, all children can experience success and grow!

Why would you hang a commercial poster, cartoon character, or plastic cardboard animal drawn by an adult when you can hang an original—a one-of-a-kind—by a very special child in your school? You'll find you will enjoy looking at the children's art much more than art by an anonymous adult, and the children will, too!

Art Gallery

Displaying children's art attractively reflects the importance of their work.

Artist's Canvas

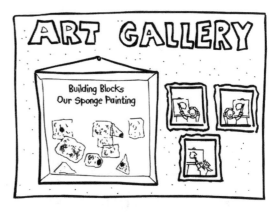

Materials
- [ ] artist's canvas (available at craft and art shops)
- [ ] paints, brushes
- [ ] collage materials

Directions Let small groups of children plan how they would like to paint the canvas. (Car painting, string painting, gadget prints, sponge prints, tissue collage, glue painting, and body prints are a few ideas.) Encourage children to give a title to their canvas, and then label the picture along with the artists' names.

Variations Photograph children in the process of creating their canvas and display the photo beside the finished product.

Purchase large picture frames and rotate children's paintings in them.

Arrange several plastic box frames on a wall. Rotate children's stories and drawings in the frames.

Pedestals

Materials
- [ ] plastic crate, stool, or cardboard box
- [ ] 1–2 yards of velvet, satin, taffeta, or other fabric

Directions Drape the fabric over the crate, stool, or box in loose folds. Display sculptures or three-dimensional projects on the pedestal.

Variations Display student-made puppets by standing them up on detergent bottles.

Use an artist's easel to display different projects and paintings.

Computer Displays

Materials
- [ ] computer
- [ ] digital camera
- [ ] scanner

Directions Prepare a computer slideshow that can be shown on a classroom computer. Using the digital camera, take photos of children creating or holding their masterpieces. Scan art done on paper and include those pieces of art in the slideshow.

Variation Make a slideshow for each child throughout the year, and give a CD of the slideshow to the child's parents at the end of the year.

Folding Gallery

Materials
- [ ] folding display board
- [ ] markers
- [ ] construction paper
- [ ] push pins

Directions Use a folding display board for children's artwork, science projects, and other school projects. Write information about the work on construction paper and use push pins to attach the paper to the board. This will allow the display board to be used many times.

Variations Have each child use a display board to present a school project.

Use the display board outside the classroom to highlight a different child's work each week.

Hang-Ups

Materials
- [ ] clothesline
- [ ] clothespins (spring-type)

Directions Attach the clothesline low on a wall in the classroom or the hallway. As children finish paintings, drawings, or other work, let them hang their pictures on the line.

Variations Let each child decorate a clothespin with her name. Children can practice identifying their names when they hang up or take down their pictures.

Use the clothesline for learning activities, such as hanging numerals in order or putting letters in alphabetical order.

Four-Sided Display

Materials   ☐ large appliance box
☐ paint, paintbrushes
☐ tape

Directions   Let children help paint the box. Tape their pictures to all four sides and display the box in an open area.

Labeling

Materials   ☐ index cards
☐ pens, pencils

Directions   Have children dictate how they made their different creations. Post the index cards with their explanations next to their artwork.

Variation   Older children can write their own descriptions or stories about their art projects.

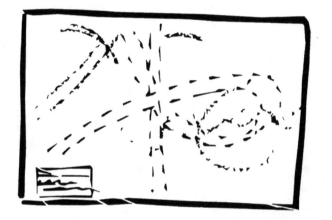

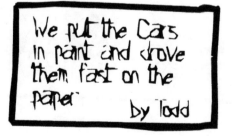

We put the Cars in paint and drove them fast on the paper
by Todd

Marvelous Murals

A mural is a wonderful project that encourages children to work together. Murals can be created with a wide variety of materials, and they provide an interesting focus on classroom walls and hallways.

Relate murals to a unit of study, season, or special interest of the children. Vary paint colors, and experiment with different types of paper and fabric.

When working on murals, hang the paper on the wall, put it on the floor, place it on a large table, or hang it from the playground fence.

Attach labels to murals that tell how children made them, or let children dictate a story about the process. It's also interesting to take a photograph of children working on the project to hang by the finished product.

Add borders to murals to create frames; then hang the murals at children's eye level.

Dinosaur Mural

Materials
- [ ] construction paper
- [ ] paint
- [ ] glue
- [ ] dinosaur books
- [ ] markers
- [ ] butcher paper
- [ ] scissors
- [ ] index cards

Directions During a unit of study on dinosaurs, have children create a dinosaur mural. Have each child choose a dinosaur to research. Each child should choose a different dinosaur. Children can use books to research different dinosaurs and the environment they lived in. Children should use construction paper, paint, and markers to create the environment on the butcher paper, and then make the dinosaurs on top of the environment background.

Give each child an index card, and have each child write facts about their dinosaur, such as its size and weight, how it moved, body features, what it ate, and how it defended itself against predators. Have children attach their index cards to the mural next to their dinosaurs.

Variations Use this mural idea for other science concepts such as the water cycle, weather, volcanoes, biomes, etc.

Use this mural for social studies concepts such as families, neighborhoods, states, countries, etc.

Bubble Painting

Materials
- [ ] bottle of bubbles
- [ ] food coloring
- [ ] butcher paper

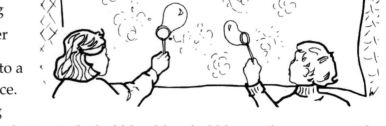

Directions Tape the paper to a playground fence. Add several big squirts of food coloring to the bubbles; blow bubbles on the paper, watch them pop, and make designs.

Animal Tracks

Materials
☐ toy animals (zoo, dinosaurs, etc.)
☐ paint
☐ pie pans
☐ butcher paper

Directions Pour paint into pie pans; dip animals' feet into the paint and let them "walk" across the paper. Play a guessing game to determine which animals made the different prints.

Variation Dip washable dolls or action figures in paint and walk them on paper.

STEP IT UP Have children group animal footprints on their paper according to the habitat where each animal can be found. Ask children to describe the habitat where each animal lives.

Crayon Bundles

Materials
☐ crayons
☐ rubber bands
☐ butcher paper

Directions Wrap rubber bands around three or four crayons to make bundles. Draw with bundles on the paper.

Variation Play music while children draw.

STEP IT UP Have children bundle crayons that are the same color (specifically one bundle of red, one of yellow, and one of blue). Have them draw with one color bundle on top of another to see what new color is made.

Picture Collage

Materials
- ☐ magazines
- ☐ glue, scissors
- ☐ butcher paper

Directions Have children cut out magazine pictures of different kinds of people and glue them onto the paper.

Variation Use magazine pictures to make murals of different kinds of homes, animals, foods, etc.

Math Mural

Materials
- ☐ construction paper
- ☐ glue, scissors
- ☐ markers, crayons
- ☐ butcher paper
- ☐ variety of geometric figures for tracing

Directions Tape the paper to a low wall. Have children trace and cut out geometric figures from construction paper. Children should glue their figures to the paper and use crayons or markers to label each figure.

Rebus Story Mural

Materials
- ☐ construction paper
- ☐ crayons, markers
- ☐ scissors, glue
- ☐ butcher paper

Directions Use a story that the class has written together recently. Rewrite that story on butcher paper, leaving blank areas for pictures to create a rebus story. Have children create the pictures on construction paper and glue them to the butcher paper to complete the story.

Recycle Mural

Materials ☐ recycle logo
☐ recyclable objects
☐ glue
☐ butcher paper

Directions Make a mural of the recycle logo and objects that can be recycled. (This is a great idea for Earth Week.)

STEP IT UP Have children add drawings to the mural to show ways that they recycle. For example, children might draw themselves putting items in a recycling bin or reusing a plastic bottle for an art project.

Story Setting Painting

Materials ☐ paint
☐ butcher paper

Directions Have children paint the setting from one of their favorite stories. Children can paint the main character from the story on the setting.

Collage Mural

Materials ☐ yarn, fabric, ribbon, lace, and other collage materials
☐ glue
☐ butcher paper or poster board

Directions Let children glue various objects onto the paper or poster board to create a colorful mural.

Variations Make a collage with tissue paper, wallpaper, construction paper scraps, etc.

Mother Nature Mural

Materials ☐ natural objects (leaves, flowers, feathers, sticks, etc.)

☐ glue

☐ large paper

Directions Glue the natural objects onto the paper. Adapt to the season by using colorful leaves in the fall or flowers in the spring.

Concept Murals

Materials ☐ magazines

☐ glue

☐ scissors

☐ crayons and markers

☐ butcher paper

Directions Have children cut out pictures or draw objects relating to a concept. For example, they could do a "blue mural" with pictures of blue objects. They could also make a mural of objects beginning with a particular letter, or they could cut out pictures of a certain shape.

 **STEP IT UP** Have children further categorize the items they include on their murals. Children can sort items by size, color, shape, texture, etc.

Rubber Band Brush

Materials ☐ rubber bands

☐ pipe cleaners

☐ pie pans, paint

☐ butcher paper

Directions String 20 to 30 rubber bands on a pipe cleaner, and then twist the pipe cleaner into a handle. Children can dip the rubber bands in pie pans of paint, and then brush them onto the paper.

Flour and Salt Paint

Materials
- ☐ flour
- ☐ salt
- ☐ tempera paint, brushes
- ☐ poster board or heavy paper

Directions Mix equal parts of flour and salt. Stir in tempera paint to make a thick consistency. Apply to heavy paper with brushes, fingers, or cotton swabs.

Postage Stamp Mural

Materials
- ☐ used postage stamps
- ☐ glue
- ☐ poster board cut in an unusual shape

Directions Ask children to save postage stamps they receive at home. Let children glue the stamps to the poster board as they bring them to school. Encourage children to identify the postmarks and stamps of different countries, cities, and states.

Habitat Mural

Materials
- ☐ paints, brushes, markers, crayons
- ☐ construction paper scraps
- ☐ collage materials
- ☐ glue, scissors
- ☐ large butcher paper

Directions Let children work together to paint different habitats, such as a rain forest, desert, arctic area, ocean, forest, etc. After they paint the background for their habitat, they can draw and cut animals out of the construction paper and glue them to the mural. They can also hang vines from the ceiling, make rocks from crumpled sacks, hang snowflakes, add a CD for sound, and so forth.

Create a Collage

Collages invite children to create, construct, and experiment as they develop small motor skills, plan, and make choices. Collages are always interesting because everyone's is different!

Materials ☐ Almost anything that's inexpensive and plentiful can be used to make a collage.

Try some of the following:

rice	used postage stamps	cotton
tissue paper	craft sticks	buttons, lace
greeting cards	fabric scraps	dried beans
shells	foam peanuts	magazines, catalogs
cupcake liners	colored sand	toothpicks
wallpaper	fish gravel	pasta
leaves, flowers	brochures	yarn
(colored with	straws	feathers
dry tempera)	wrapping paper	beads

Collages can be made on:

paper plates	paper (all kinds)
plastic lids	grocery sacks
contact paper	cardboard

To attach objects to a collage, use:

glue	masking tape
glue sticks	cellophane tape
colored glue	liquid starch
(colored with food coloring)	

Let children tear paper, or use scissors, a hole punch, or precut shapes.

HINT Limit the number of choices depending on the age of the children. Put collage materials in clear cartons, muffin pans, butter tubs, or separate containers.

Fabric Collage

Materials ☐ fabric scraps

☐ ribbon, lace, rickrack, buttons, and other sewing notions

☐ glue, paper

Directions Cut up the fabric and arrange it on the paper. Decorate it with buttons and other trim.

Variations Make a fabric collage on burlap.

Decorate a box lid or oatmeal box with buttons and trim for a gift.

Letter Collage

Materials ☐ poster board

☐ magazines

☐ glue, scissors

☐ collage materials

Directions Cut giant letters out of the poster board. Have children cut out objects beginning with the appropriate sound to glue on each letter, or decorate with collage materials beginning with that sound. (For example, glue feathers on the "f ," ribbon scraps on the "r," yarn on the "y," colored cottonballs on the "c," etc.)

STEP IT UP Have children use the letters they make to form consonant blends, CVC words, CVCC words, etc. Focus on phonics skills currently being taught.

Concept Collage

Materials ☐ poster board

☐ paper, glue, scissors

☐ catalogs, magazines

Directions Have children cut out objects that relate to a particular concept or skill. They could make a green collage from pictures of things that are green, a "p" collage of objects that start with a "p," a shape collage of circles, triangles, squares, etc.

Zipper-Bag Collage

Materials ☐ plastic zipper bags
☐ tissue paper (variety of colors)

Directions Let children tear tissue paper into small pieces and put the pieces in zipper bags. Tape the zipper bags to a sunny window or staple them to a bulletin board.

Variation Take children on a nature walk and let them fill the zipper bags with leaves, flowers, etc.

Family Collage

Materials ☐ family photos
☐ magazines
☐ glue, scissors
☐ paper

Directions Ask children to bring in some family photos and old magazines. Have children find pictures in magazines that show things they like to do with their families. Have children glue those pictures and their family photos to paper.

Variation Put all of the collages together into a class scrapbook.

Pop-Up Collage

Materials ☐ construction paper (whole sheets and strips)
☐ scissors, glue
☐ old magazines

Directions Have children cut out pictures of things they enjoy doing from magazines. Have children fold the construction paper strips accordion-style and glue them to the backs of the pictures. Then have them glue those to the construction paper sheets so the pictures "pop-up."

Texture Collage

Materials ☐ cotton, bubblewrap, velvet, felt, sandpaper, carpet scraps, burlap, and other objects with different textures

☐ glue

☐ cardboard scraps

Directions Arrange textured objects on the cardboard and glue them in place.

Nature Collage

Materials ☐ wood scraps

☐ glue

☐ natural objects

Directions Take children on a nature walk to collect leaves, seeds, small rocks, feathers, moss, and other treasures. Have them glue the objects onto wood scraps.

Variations Let children glue natural objects to tree bark, logs, or paper plates.

Vary the nature collage for the season. Create an autumn collage with colored leaves; a winter collage with sticks, dead leaves, and evergreens; or a spring collage with flowers and leaves.

Tissue Paper Collage

Materials ☐ tissue paper

☐ scissors

☐ white paper

☐ spray bottle of water

Directions Cut or tear the tissue paper into small pieces; then arrange it on white paper. Spray with water. Dry. Peel off the tissue paper and see the unusual design deposited by the tissue paper.

Variation Glue small pieces of tissue paper to wax paper with liquid starch. Dry. Trim the edges and hang from the window as a sun catcher.

Newspaper Art

Using newspapers for art projects is a perfect way to teach children about recycling. In addition to saving money, newspapers provide a large space on which little hands can create.

Pounce Painting

Materials
- ☐ fabric scraps cut in 5" circles
- ☐ craft sticks
- ☐ cotton balls
- ☐ rubber bands
- ☐ paint
- ☐ newspapers

Directions   Place the fabric on the table and put three cotton balls in the center of each piece. Wrap the fabric around the end of a craft stick and tie a rubber band in place. Dip it in paint; then "pounce" on the newspaper.

Variations   Tie a jingle bell around the pouncer so it makes noise as you paint. Make pouncers large or small by varying the number of cotton balls.

Put small pieces of sponge in spring clothespins and use as paintbrushes.

Sponge Prints

Materials
- ☐ sponges cut in various shapes
- ☐ pie pans, paint
- ☐ newspapers

Directions   Pour a small amount of paint into the pie pans. Let children dip sponges in the paint; then print with them on the newspaper.

Variations   Use sponge balls.

Cut sponges into holiday shapes or objects that relate to a theme.

Gadget Painting

Materials ☐ plastic berry baskets, toothbrushes, spools, plastic forks, cookie cutters, and other kitchen utensils

☐ paint, pie pans

☐ newspapers

Directions Put paint in the pie pans. Dip the gadgets in the paint; then print with them on the newspaper.

Variation Instead of the gadgets, use pine boughs, sticks, feathers, toy animals, and other objects.

Bubblewrap Painting

Materials ☐ plastic bubblewrap

☐ paint, brushes

☐ newspapers

Directions Paint a picture or design on the bubblewrap. Put a sheet of newspaper on top of the bubblewrap and rub. Lift to reveal the design.

Scrap Paper Collage

Materials ☐ scrap paper (wallpaper, construction paper, tissue paper, wrapping paper, etc.)

☐ scissors, glue

☐ newspapers

Directions Cut the scrap paper into different shapes and glue it onto the newspaper.

Newspaper Creatures

Materials ☐ newspapers
☐ markers

Directions Starting on the fold, tear an abstract shape from the newspaper. Open it up and turn it all around until you see a "creature." Add details with markers or construction paper scraps.

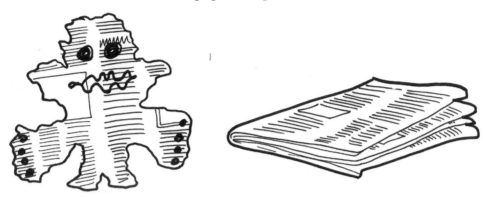

STEP IT UP Have each child write or dictate a story with a newspaper creature as the main character. Encourage children to make other newspaper creatures to include in the story. Invite children to share their stories with the class.

Three-Dimensional Art

Three-dimensional art provides children with a different perspective and challenge.

Clay

Materials
- ☐ modeling clay
- ☐ toothpicks
- ☐ beans, yarn, and collage materials

Directions Let children mold people and objects with the clay, and add detail with toothpicks, beads, etc.

Food Sculpture

Materials
- ☐ pretzels, toothpicks, raisins, nut-free cereal, celery sticks, shredded carrots, cream cheese, crackers, etc.
- ☐ plates, napkins, craft sticks

Directions After children have washed their hands, give them some of the above foods and materials to create a sculpture. Then eat!

Paper Sculpture

Materials
- ☐ scrap paper
- ☐ cardboard cut into squares
- ☐ glue or tape

Directions Children can fold, twist, twirl, roll, bend, and tear the paper, and then glue or tape it to the cardboard to make it stand up.

Filter Colors

Materials ☐ coffee filters ☐ black marker
☐ water ☐ dropper

Directions Draw lines on a coffee filter with black marker. Drop water on the black lines. Watch the colors that spread from the black lines. Explain to children that the color black is made up of all colors. Adding the water shows all of the colors that form black. Display children's coffee filters on a bulletin board about colors.

Cardboard Rollers

Materials ☐ cardboard rollers (from toilet paper)
☐ construction paper
☐ scissors, glue
☐ crayons, markers
☐ junk box

Directions Encourage children to use their imagination as they turn the toilet paper rolls into people, trees, animals, etc.

STEP IT UP Give children rulers. Have them measure the length of their cardboard rollers. Have children write their measurements on index cards and display them with their cardboard rollers.

Foil Friends

Materials ☐ aluminum foil

Directions Tear off a piece of aluminum foil approximately 12" long. Tear in the middle, ⅓ of the way up from the bottom. Make two tears down from the top ⅓ of the way as shown. Squeeze the two bottom sections to be legs, and then squeeze the top side sections for arms; the middle section can become the head. Continue molding the foil into a character.

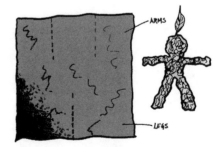

Variations Make a cape from fabric and you'll have a superhero.

Mold a feather in the top and you'll have a knight in shining armor.

Plastic Foam Creation

Recycle foam packing into unique sculptures and wall hangings.

Materials
- ☐ large piece of foam packing material (used to ship computers and televisions)
- ☐ toothpicks
- ☐ tissue paper
- ☐ colored glue
- ☐ glitter, ribbon
- ☐ pipe cleaners

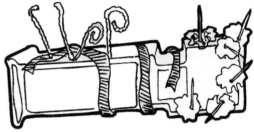

Directions   Give small groups of children the above materials and challenge them to create a sculpture using the packing material as a base. (You might need to demonstrate how to secure the tissue paper and ribbon with toothpicks and pipe cleaners.) Decorate the sculpture with glue and glitter. Hang it from the wall or display on a podium or shelf.

Variation   Children can make individual sculptures with foam plates, cups, pipe cleaners, aluminum foil, and foam peanuts.

Moving Sculpture

What an exciting way to involve all the children in your classroom—creating a giant sculpture that is constantly evolving!

Materials
- ☐ corrugated cardboard boxes (any size)—one for each child
- ☐ tape
- ☐ large paintbrushes (purchase inexpensive ones like painters use)
- ☐ red, yellow, blue paint (BioColor works well, as it does not rub off)
- ☐ newspapers
- ☐ plastic containers for paint (margarine tubs)
- ☐ smocks

Directions
Ask each child to bring in a cardboard box, or ask an office supply store to save boxes for you. Tape the boxes shut. Cover the working area with newspapers and provide smocks for children. Pour the paint into the plastic containers; let each child paint his or her box with the primary colors. Dry. The next day, encourage children to paint designs on their boxes. They can also print patterns on them with sponges. Dry. Let children freely explore building giant sculptures with their boxes. Reinforce what happens when everyone works together.

Variations
Redesign the sculpture. How tall can they make it? How long? Can they build a tunnel they can crawl under? Can they march around it? Can they think of a title for their sculpture?

Place the boxes in the lobby or hall and let parents, children, and staff move the boxes around.

Play the boxes like drums.

Take them outside on a dry day to play with.

STEP IT UP
Have children choose one side of their boxes. Give each child a ruler, and show them how to measure each edge of that side to find the perimeter of the side.

Wall Sculpture

This could go in a real art museum, but children will have fun creating it and seeing it in their school.

Materials
☐ foam board
☐ glue gun
☐ plastic containers and "junk" (egg cartons, bottles, packages, cake trays, detergent bottles, beads, old toys, lids, etc.)
☐ spray paint (must adhere to polystyrene and plastic)

Directions
Have children collect the objects and arrange them on the board. Glue the objects in place. (An adult may need to do this with a glue gun.) Spray paint. Hang on the wall.

Variations
Allow children to paint the sculptures with paint that will adhere to plastic (e.g., BioColor).

Glue yarn, tinsel, tissue paper, and other objects to the sculpture after it is painted.

Create a plastic dragon by gluing recycled containers to a strip of felt as shown.

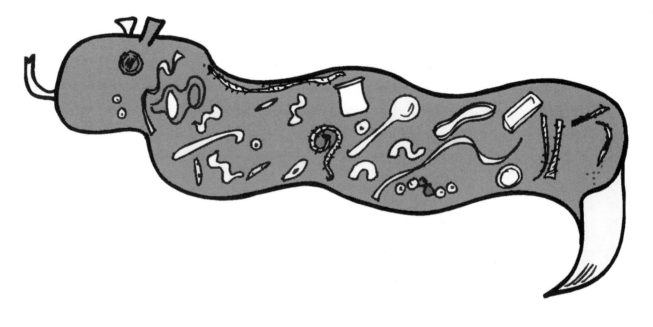

Roller Coaster Sculpture

Children will enjoy creating their own looping and plunging roller coaster models.

Materials
- ☐ art tape
- ☐ cardboard
- ☐ scissors

Directions   Have children create their own roller coasters using art tape. Children can cut lengths of art tape, which has glue on one side and is very sturdy. Children can make hills and loop-the-loops by licking and sticking the tape to the cardboard.

Variations   Give children construction paper to make roller coaster cars and people riding on the roller coaster.

Have children measure the height of each hill on their roller coasters with a ruler.

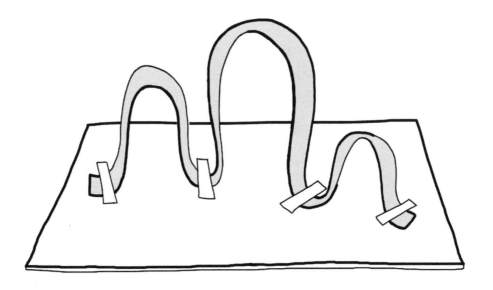

Sand Castle Sculptures

The creative juices will flow as children build sand castles that reflect each individual's imagination and style.

Materials
- ☐ self-hardening clay
- ☐ modeling tools (craft sticks, plastic utensils, toothpicks, etc.)
- ☐ fine sand of various colors (sand can be colored by mixing with dry tempera paint)
- ☐ decorative items such as shells, glitter, etc.
- ☐ pictures of sand castles and real castles

Directions
Show children the pictures of sand castles and real castles. Discuss the different parts of the castles. Give each child clay, and have children model their own castles. Help children to gently press the colored sand in the sides of their castles. Have children add detail and decorative items to their castles.

Variations
Have children put their sand castles together to build a sand castle city. The city should include roads, parks, etc.

Have three to four children work as a group to build one sand castle.

Dynamic Dioramas

Dioramas are a unique way for individuals or cooperative learning groups to display their creativity.

Materials
- ☐ cardboard boxes (shoe boxes for individuals; corrugated cardboard boxes for group projects)
- ☐ paper scraps
- ☐ paint, paintbrushes
- ☐ glue, scissors, tape, string
- ☐ pipe cleaners, clay, foil, craft sticks, etc.
- ☐ collage materials, junk

Directions   Ask children to think of a favorite scene. It could be from a book, a place in their community, a period in history, a celebration, a habitat, etc. Let them paint the inside of the box and create a three-dimensional scene using various art media. Objects can be suspended from the top of the box with string. Stand up characters and props with clay or glue. Characters and animals can be made from paper, clay, or papier-mâché. Natural objects (rocks, sticks, leaves), small boxes, toys, and junk can also be used to build a diorama.

Variation   Stack several dioramas on top of each other to create a fascinating display.

HINT   This project can take several days or even weeks to create, so provide children with a place to work and store their dioramas.

Surprise Picture Frame

Children will have fun creating these surprise pictures and making a "surprise" display.

Materials
- ☐ construction paper (2 sheets per child)
- ☐ natural objects (seeds, leaves, flowers, feathers, pebbles, shells, etc.)
- ☐ glue
- ☐ scissors
- ☐ pencil

Directions   Take children on a nature walk and let them collect natural objects. (Challenge them to find things that are lightweight.)

Put the natural objects in the middle of one sheet of paper. Take the second sheet and cut diagonal lines out from the middle to within one inch of the corners as shown. Put glue around the edges of the second sheet, and then place it on top of the sheet with the natural objects. Take each point and roll it back from the middle around a pencil. (This should make a pop-up frame around the objects.)

Variation   Stick objects on the sticky side of a sheet of contact paper. Place a curled construction paper frame on top of it.

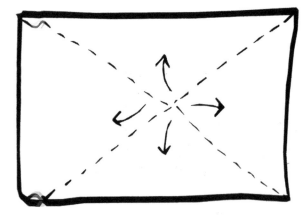

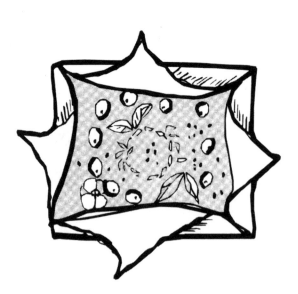

Mobiles

Mobiles allow children to plan, construct, and experiment with ordinary materials in a unique way. Mobiles also add interest to your classroom.

Coat Hanger Story Mobile

Materials
- ☐ coat hangers
- ☐ crayons, markers
- ☐ scissors, hole punch
- ☐ construction paper
- ☐ yarn or string

Directions   Have children choose a story they have read recently. Color and cut out from the construction paper various objects that represent the story. Children should make objects that represent the main character, setting, plot, problem, and solution. Punch holes in the shapes and tie them onto the coat hanger with string or yarn. Hang the mobile from the ceiling.

Variations   Relate mobiles to a season, holiday, or theme.

Let children cut out the letters in their names and hang the letters on mobiles.

Earth Day Mobile

Materials
- ☐ coat hangers
- ☐ tape
- ☐ string or yarn
- ☐ trash (candy wrapper, foil, plastic bags, etc.)

Directions   Have children bring in cleaned, recycled materials from home. Tape the trash to the coat hangers or tie it on with string.

Nature Mobile

Materials
- ☐ stick or tree branch
- ☐ natural objects (leaves, feathers, shells, seed pods, pine cones, flowers, etc.)
- ☐ string or yarn

Directions
- ☐ Attach a string to the stick for hanging; tie on the other natural objects.

STEP IT UP

Have children write a sentence or two on index cards telling about each object on their mobile. Have children attach the index cards to the corresponding objects on their mobiles using string.

Spiral

Materials
- ☐ paper plates
- ☐ scissors, hole punch
- ☐ construction paper scraps
- ☐ string or yarn

Directions   Cut each paper plate into a spiral as illustrated. Cut out objects from the construction paper and tie them onto the spiral with string or yarn. Hang the mobile from a hole punched in the center of the spiral.

Banners, Banderas, and Windsocks

Halls and rooms can get "hung up" with these ideas.

Banners

Materials
- ☐ coat hangers
- ☐ construction paper
- ☐ scissors, glue
- ☐ paint, markers, and crayons

Directions Fold the construction paper in half and hang it over the hanger. Cut the bottom edge in a zigzag, curve, or other design. Decorate the construction paper with paints, markers, or crayons and glue it to the hanger.

Variations Make pennants from felt and decorate with felt scraps.

Let each child make an "all about me" banner, or a banner to illustrate his favorite book or sports team.

Banderas

Materials
- ☐ construction or tissue paper cut in rectangles
- ☐ scissors
- ☐ string, tape

Directions Have children fold their paper several times. Show them how to cut little pieces out of the folds (much as if they were making snowflakes). Tie string across the classroom or hallway; tape the banderas to the string.

Windsocks

Materials ☐ construction paper (10" × 18" rectangles)
☐ tissue paper
☐ paints, markers, crayons
☐ hole punch, scissors
☐ glue, stapler
☐ string

Directions Decorate the paper horizontally. Turn it over and glue strips of tissue paper (12" to 18" long) to the bottom as shown. Bring the sides together to make a cylinder and staple. Punch three holes evenly spaced on the top edge. Tie a 12" piece of string to each hole; bring the ends of the string together and knot.

Variation Make mini-windsocks from toilet paper rolls. Decorate with markers and add tissue paper streamers.

STEP IT UP

Have children do other weather-related activities, such as determining how far away a thunderstorm is. The next time there is a thunderstorm, give each child a stopwatch. Have children start the stopwatches when they see the lightning, and stop them when they hear the thunder. For every five seconds counted, the storm is one mile away. Have children divide the number of seconds by five to get the number of miles. Help children with tougher division, or allow them to use a calculator as needed. Explain that the sound of thunder is heard after the lightning is seen because light travels faster than sound through air.

Paper Chains

Paper chains demonstrate connectedness and can be used to reinforce learning while they decorate the classroom.

Materials
- ☐ construction paper cut in strips
- ☐ glue or stapler
- ☐ crayons, markers

Friendship Chain — Ask each child to decorate a strip of paper with his name and designs. Glue or staple the strips together to make a friendship chain, and hang it in the classroom.

Countdown Chain — Make a chain using the number of links equal to the number of days left until a vacation, field trip, party, or other celebration. Remove a link each day until the special day arrives.

Diary Chain — At the end of each day, have children tell you what they liked best or learned that day. Write what they say on a strip of paper and date it. Each day, add to the chain and hang it around the classroom as it grows. (You might want to use a different color paper each month.)

Seasonal Decorations — Make chains to decorate the classroom for different seasons or holidays. For example, red and white could be used in February, or orange and black could be used in October. Hang chains around windows or from the ceiling.

Rainbow Chain — Make paper chains of different colors in the rainbow. Loop them from the ceiling to create a rainbow in the classroom.

Family Chain — Let each family in your school decorate a strip of paper; then create a large chain that represents the entire school.

Crumpled Paper Sculpture

Crumpled paper can be sculpted into trees, animals, and other interesting objects.

Materials
- ☐ brown butcher paper
- ☐ construction paper
- ☐ paper plates
- ☐ toilet paper rolls
- ☐ tissue paper, pipe cleaners
- ☐ string or yarn
- ☐ scissors, glue, markers, crayons, tape, stapler

Directions   Crumple the butcher paper several times until it is pliable and can be molded. Sculpt it into a tree trunk with branches; then staple it to a bulletin board or tape it to a wall. Cut leaves or vines out of construction paper and add them to the tree. Make other objects to hang from the branches:

Snakes—Color paper plates, and then cut them into spirals.

Monkeys—Add heads, arms, legs, and a tail to toilet paper rolls to make little monkeys.

Butterflies—Make butterflies by folding 8" squares of tissue paper back and forth accordion style. Twist a pipe cleaner around the middle of the fold; ruffle tissue paper to make wings.

Birds—Use construction paper to make birds.

Flowers—Take four pieces of tissue paper cut in 6" squares. Fold back and forth in accordion folds and twist a pipe cleaner around the middle of the folded shape. Separate layers to open into a flower.

Variation   Mold rocks, mountains, animals, vehicles, homes, or other objects that relate to a season or unit of study out of crumpled paper. Let children add detail and decorate.

Giant Animals

Children will enjoy working together to make these giant creatures and pretend characters.

Materials
- ☐ butcher paper
- ☐ paint, chalk, markers, crayons, or collage materials
- ☐ scissors, stapler
- ☐ newspaper

Directions Lay a piece of butcher paper on the floor; then place a second sheet on top. Sketch the shape of a large animal or character on one side, and then cut through both thicknesses to make two like shapes. Let children paint and decorate both sides with paint, chalk, markers, crayons, or collage materials. Staple the edges together ¾ of the way around. Ask children to tear up small strips of newspaper and stuff them inside the shape. Staple the opening closed. Hang on a wall or from the ceiling.

Variation Make giant shapes that relate to a theme or interest of the children. Let each child make his or her own giant shape. It could be a snowman, butterfly, dinosaur, etc. Provide paints, fabric scraps, markers, wallpaper, and other collage materials to decorate it with. Cut large objects out of foam board and let the children decorate them with markers and collage materials. Hang from walls, doors, or the ceiling.

STEP IT UP Have children create giant animals that are related to a unit of study in science. For example, they can create ocean animals as part of an ocean unit. Have books available for children to use for research on the ocean animals they choose.

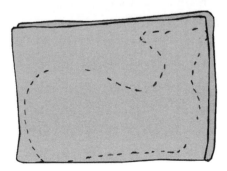

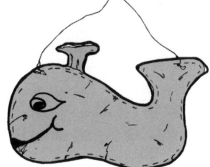

Classroom Quilts

Social skills will flourish as children work together to create a quilt for their classroom. Quilts also reflect community effort and the beauty that evolves as individuals work together.

Materials
- ☐ fabric crayons
- ☐ paper, iron
- ☐ tape
- ☐ squares of inexpensive white cloth or muslin

Directions Have children draw designs on a piece of paper with the fabric crayons. (Remind them to press hard and make their designs as colorful as possible.) Place the picture on the fabric face down; iron with a medium iron, pressing hard until the color transfers. Sew or tape the squares together. Add backing if you desire.

HINT If you write on the paper, you must do so backwards so that when it is ironed it will be correct.

Burlap Stitchery

Materials
- ☐ squares of burlap
- ☐ plastic needles
- ☐ yarn, scissors

Directions Let children sew original designs on a square of burlap with yarn. Sew sections together or use cloth tape to hold them in place.

All of Us

Materials
- ☐ paper cut in 8" squares
- ☐ markers and crayons
- ☐ hole punch
- ☐ yarn

Directions Give each child a square on which to draw a self-portrait. Provide children with markers and crayons in body colors. Punch holes in the four corners of each picture; tie the pictures together with yarn.

Weaving

Materials
- ☐ long strips of paper (3" × 36")
- ☐ crayons, markers

Directions Let children decorate strips of paper and weave them together.

Food Color Dip

Materials
- ☐ paper towels
- ☐ food coloring
- ☐ cups
- ☐ cloth tape

Directions Fill four cups ¼ full with water. Add several squirts of food coloring to each cup. Take each paper towel and fold it four times into a small square. Dip each corner in a different color. (Just dip the tip as the towel absorbs the color.) Unfold the towels and let dry. Tape the towels together or staple them to a bulletin board.

Variation Let children bundle up sections of the towel and wrap a rubber band around each bundle. Dip bundles in different colors to create a tie-dye effect.

Cultural Designs

Materials ☐ squares of white fabric or muslin
☐ markers

Directions Have children research their heritage. Ask each child to design a fabric square to reflect a country that some of his ancestors came from. Sew the squares together.

Variation Decorate pieces of white poster board cut in 2" squares, and tape them to a wall to create a quilt.

Crazy Quilt

Materials ☐ pictures, paintings, printing, collages, and other art
☐ projects children have left at school without their names
☐ poster board
☐ glue

Directions Cut the art and projects into geometric shapes and arrange on the poster board. Glue in place. Add a border to give it a finished look.

Puzzle

Materials ☐ large piece of corrugated cardboard or poster board
☐ scissors
☐ markers, crayons

Directions Cut the cardboard into puzzle pieces. Make enough so each child in your class can have a piece of the puzzle to decorate with markers or crayons. Glue or tape the pieces together.

"Me" Pictures

Children love themselves and will enjoy drawing their pictures with these ideas.

Look At Me

Materials
- ☐ mirror
- ☐ paper
- ☐ flesh tone crayons, markers, and paints

Directions Hang a mirror by the art easel so children can look at themselves as they draw their portraits.

Happy Portraits

Materials
- ☐ construction paper
- ☐ crayons and markers
- ☐ wiggly eyes, buttons, and other collage materials
- ☐ scissors, glue
- ☐ pencils

Directions Let children draw pictures of themselves doing something that makes them happy, such as playing a favorite sport or reading a favorite book. Have children write a paragraph to describe what they're doing in the picture and how they feel when they are doing it.

Friend Portraits

Materials
- ☐ paper
- ☐ flesh tone crayons and markers

Directions Divide the class into pairs. Have partners sit in facing chairs as they draw each other's pictures.

When I Grow Up

Materials
- [ ] butcher paper
- [ ] crayons, paint, markers
- [ ] collage materials
- [ ] glue, scissors

Directions
Have children lie on the butcher paper as a friend traces around their bodies. Cut out. Decorate with crayons and collage materials to show what they want to be when they grow up.

Silhouettes

Materials
- [ ] black and white construction paper
- [ ] pencil, glue, scissors
- [ ] source of light, such as an overhead projector, bright lamp, flashlight

Directions
Tape a sheet of black paper to the wall. Set up the light source several feet away from the paper so the light shines on the paper. Ask one child at a time to sit in a chair between the paper and the light, facing sideways so his or her shadow is reflected on the paper. Trace around the child's silhouette with a pencil and cut out the silhouette. Glue the silhouette onto the white sheet of paper.

Variations
Hang silhouettes on a bulletin board or wall and let children guess whom each shadow represents.

Make white silhouettes and allow children to paint them with body-colored paints.

Have children write words on their silhouettes that describe themselves or things they do well.

Artistic Impressions

Enhance aesthetic appreciation and expose children to famous artists with this idea.

Materials
- ☐ old art books (available at used book stores, college book stores, garage sales, etc.)
- ☐ bulletin board or poster board
- ☐ glue, scissors
- ☐ construction paper

Directions Choose an artist and cut out several of his or her pictures. Mount the pictures attractively on construction paper and arrange them on a bulletin board with the artist's name. Introduce children to the "artist of the month" by giving a little biographical information about the artist. Tell children the titles of the pictures and discuss the materials used to create them. Encourage children's comments about how the pictures make them feel. Introduce a new artist to children each month.

Variations Art calendars and postcards also work well for this project.

Make a "Big Book of Artists" by cutting pieces of poster board in half. Put pictures by artists you have introduced to children on the poster board; fasten the pieces together with book rings. Look through the book with children to see if they can identify different artists' work.

Invite an artist to visit your classroom, or take children on a field trip to an art museum.

STEP IT UP Have children choose an artist to research in the school library and on the Internet. Have children write a paragraph about the artist or give a brief presentation to the class, including samples of the artist's work.

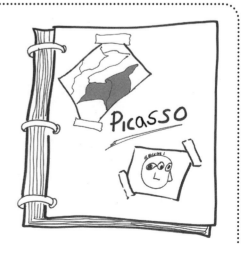

The Great Frame-Up

Take the time to display children's work with some of these simple frames.

Bits and Pieces

Materials
- ☐ mat board or poster board
- ☐ utility knife
- ☐ children's artwork
- ☐ tape

Directions Cut various geometric or abstract shapes out of the poster board with the utility knife. Tape a different piece of art behind each opening. (Label with children's names and the process used.)

Variation Add a border or mount on contrasting poster board.

Mat It

Materials
- ☐ black construction paper
- ☐ art project
- ☐ scissors
- ☐ glue
- ☐ crayons

Directions Take black construction paper the size of the art project and cut out an oval or rectangle from the center. Have each child decorate her frame using crayons. Glue this over the picture and label with the child's name and a description of how the artwork was made.

Variation Ask art or frame shops to save their mat scraps for you.

Paper Frames

Materials ☐ construction paper
☐ art project
☐ glue sticks

Directions Cut the construction paper so it is 2" to 4" longer and wider than the project to be framed. Glue the project to the middle of the construction paper; then crease in all the edges of the construction paper so they stand up and make a shadow-box frame.

Variations Use shirt boxes or gift boxes as frames for art.

Glue art to cardboard; then glue craft sticks around the edges to create a border.

Fun Frames

Materials ☐ poster board or cardboard
☐ scissors
☐ jigsaw puzzle pieces
☐ glue

Directions Cut the poster board into the shape of a frame. Let children glue old puzzle pieces to the frame. (This frame is also a great gift idea.)

Variations Have children tear pieces of construction paper and glue them onto a cardboard frame.

Children can use golf tees, natural objects, buttons, shells, and many other collage materials to decorate their frames.

Peek-A-Boo

Children will be surprised by peek-a-boo and hidden pictures.

Materials
- [ ] poster board
- [ ] fabric scraps
- [ ] tape, glue
- [ ] colorful pictures

Directions Glue four or five pictures onto the poster board. (Cut out pictures of things your children would enjoy.) Cut a piece of fabric to cover each picture. Tape the fabric to the top of each picture. Hang the peek-a-boo poster on the back of a shelf or door so children can lift the fabric and see the pictures.

Variations Play a guessing game to see if children can remember where a certain picture is hidden.

Tape a towel or blanket over a small mirror so children can play peek-a-boo and see themselves.

Place different textures for children to feel under the peek-a-boos.

Make peek-a-boo books. Glue pictures on construction paper. Cut flaps out of wallpaper and tape them over the pictures. Put several pages together to make a book.

STEP IT UP Have children write a question on the top of each flap. Then have them draw a picture and/or write a sentence under the flap to answer the question.

PART 5

Learning Centers for Child-Centered Classrooms

Centers are the most natural way to organize a classroom to enable children to become active learners.

Centers give children opportunities to make choices, explore at their own level, engage in hands-on discovery, solve problems, work with friends, use language, and be creative. Centers also allow children to move, involve a greater use of the senses, and are an effective way to use classroom materials, time, and space. Howard Gardner, author of *Multiple Intelligences*, recommends that classrooms be set up like "discovery museums." Clearly, learning centers support this theory and the child's total development by encouraging many different interests and talents. Above all, learning centers are fun and capitalize on play, which is the most meaningful way for children to learn.

Remember—with learning centers, the teacher's role is that of a facilitator. Provide children with challenges, opportunities to learn, and open-ended materials, then trust them to construct their own knowledge in their own unique ways.

Research suggests that children need large blocks of time — 45 minutes minimum — to explore learning activities and really get involved in them. Research further emphasizes the importance of carefully selecting materials and equipment that meet the developmental needs and interests of the children. With too many toys and props, children focus on the objects rather than interacting with each other. On the other hand, if there are too few materials, children will fight over toys and become aggressive.

According to the report on *Developing Early Literacy* by the National Early Literacy Panel (2008), quality literacy learning centers in early childhood classrooms can have a positive effect on a child's reading readiness. It is important that these centers include a variety of opportunities for exposure to meaningful text. Literacy can also be addressed in all of the other learning centers in the classroom.

Centers that should be available in your classroom include:

blocks/construction	writing
dramatic play	sensory play
art	music
manipulatives	large motor
science	library
math	computer

Not all of these centers have to be set up in your classroom at the same time. For example, blocks/construction and sensory play could be rotated. Other centers can easily be combined, such as science and math, and writing and computer. The library center could be combined with the quiet place (see page 53).

Consider these guidelines in arranging your classroom to create interest areas that will enhance play, social interaction, independence, and learning:*

▶ Arrange centers according to the noise and activity level. For example, quieter centers such as the library, manipulatives, and science should be grouped together, while blocks, dramatic play, and art should be in another area.

▶ Partition the classroom with shelves, bookcases, play units, and dividers to create smaller spaces. With large open areas, children are more likely to run, and to have difficulty concentrating.

▶ Provide children with at least four activities to choose from in each center. Arrange the toys so the children can easily take them out and put them back in place.

▶ Avoid clutter in centers by rotating materials.

▶ Art, sensory play, and eating areas should be on washable flooring. Carpeting in blocks, dramatic play, and the library adds warmth and will keep the noise down.

▶ Think about the natural flow and traffic patterns in the classroom. Art and sensory play should be near the sink, cubbies near the door, science by a window, music close to an electrical outlet, etc.

▶ Draw a floor plan of your classroom and cut out scaled shapes to represent furniture and equipment. Try different arrangements until you get optimal use of your space.

▶ Get down on your knees to get a "child's-eye view" of the classroom. Stand up for a "teacher's-eye view" to make sure you can supervise the children at all times.

* The National Association for the Education of Young Children (NAEYC) provides excellent criteria for setting up positive classroom environments for children in their accreditation materials. More information can be found at www.naeyc.org.

Center Management

There are many different ways to manage learning centers, and the one that is best is the one that works for you. The ages and abilities of your children, as well as your goals and philosophy, will influence your choice of strategies.

Choice Board Make a poster board with illustrations of the different centers in your classroom. (Use real photographs or pictures from school supply catalogs for this.) Make dots along the side (as shown) to represent the number of children who can play in each center. Write each child's name on a clothespin. At center time, each child may put his clothespin on the center where he would like to play. When the child wants to change centers, he needs to get his clothespin and select another area that has an empty space.

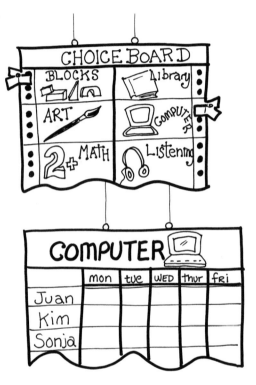

Graphs Put up a graph each week in each center with all the children's names. Have children color in their names on the graph when they go to each center.

Contracts Give each child a contract (these can be done daily or weekly) with the different centers listed. As children complete activities, they can color in the appropriate section on their contract. Older children can write a sentence or two telling about something they did in each center.

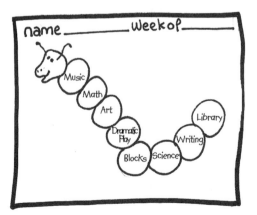

Center Necklace   Choose a different color for each center in your classroom. For example, "blocks/construction" could be brown, "library" purple, "manipulatives" red, etc. Cover a coffee can with construction paper in the appropriate color for each center and put the cans in the appropriate areas. Next, color clothespins with markers to match the centers. (You will need one of each color for every child.) Make a "center necklace" for each child with a 30" piece of ribbon or string. Have each child decorate a 3" cardboard circle with her name, punch a hole in it, and string it on her necklace. On Monday, pass out the clothespins for each center and have the children hang them on their necklaces. Explain the different activities they can do at the centers that week. As children go to different centers during the week, they take their clothespins and put them in the cans of the corresponding colors. (Have the children store their necklaces in their cubbies and wear them only at center time.) If children finish all of their centers by Friday, they get to do a special activity. This method encourages children to take responsibility for their own learning and manage their time.

Individual Conferences   Ask children individually where they would like to play and what they plan to do there. Use a puppet, play telephone, microphone, or other prop to do this. Follow up after center time by asking the children what they did or by having them draw pictures and/or write sentences in their journals.

Sign Off   Hang a list of children's names by each center and ask them to cross their names off after they have played there. They could also sign their names to a sheet of paper on a clipboard as they go to different centers.

Card Punch   Print the numerals from 1 to 4 on index cards (or use numerals that represent the number of centers in your classroom). Give each child a card with these numbers and ask him to write his name on it. Number the different centers in the classroom; as a child completes a task or finishes playing in that area, the teacher can punch a hole in the child's card next to the corresponding numeral. (Cards can be used for a week by adding more centers and numerals on index cards.)

Bracelets, Aprons, Hats, or Clothespins   Use colored bracelets, clothespins, hats, aprons, or other props children can wear as they play in a center. For example, a child who wants to play in blocks/construction could wear a construction hat; a child who wants to play in the dramatic play area could put on an apron; a child who wants to use a computer could wear a bracelet. (Have the same number of props as the number of children you want in the area at one time.)

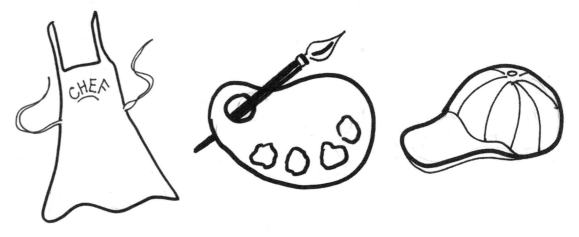

Picture Cards   Cut out pictures representative of the different centers in your classroom from school supply catalogs. (Cut out the same number of pictures for each area as children who can play in that area.) Glue the pictures to poster board cards cut in 4" squares. At center time, shuffle up the cards and have each child draw one. Each child then goes to the center on his card.

Observation   Observe children, then guide them to areas where they can enhance skills. Pair children with different abilities to play games or work on tasks so they can learn from each other. Make anecdotal notes on children's understanding of the concepts taught at different centers.

Look and See Write children's names down the left side of a poster board. Attach three small adhesive hooks beside each child's name. Cut out 3" circles and punch a hole in the top of each one. Write the names of different centers in the classroom on the circles. Each day put three different centers beside each child's name for her to complete that day. Children do the assigned centers in sequence, then are given free choice.

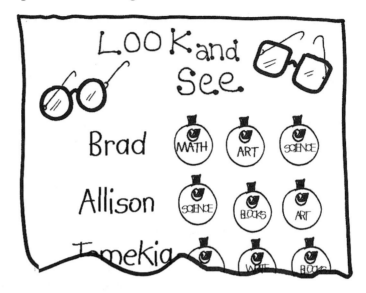

HINT Children need to work for a minimum of 45 minutes to an hour every day in learning centers in order to engage in elaborate and meaningful play.

When limiting the number of children who can play in a center at a given time, it is best to use even numbers, such as two or four.

Learning Centers Book

Children will enjoy making and reading this learning centers book. It is also an effective way to communicate with parents about developmentally appropriate practices and the value of learning through play.

Materials
- ☐ construction paper cut into 9" × 12" pieces
- ☐ photographs of the children playing in different learning centers
- ☐ scissors, glue, hole punch
- ☐ 2 book rings
- ☐ markers, crayons

Directions   Make a cover for the book called "Learning Is Fun." On each page, glue a photograph of a learning center and write a description similar to those on the following page. Hole-punch the pages and put them together with book rings. Read the book to the children, then let them "read" it to each other by telling about the pictures. Each day, allow one child to take home the book to share with his family.

Variations   Use pictures of different learning centers from school supply catalogs if you don't have photographs.

Let the children draw pictures of themselves playing in the different centers, then have them dictate what they do in each center to use as the text for the book.

Ask each child to draw a picture about what she likes best at school. Put the pages together in a book called "School Is Fun."

Learning Center Fun

Blocks/Construction In the blocks/construction center I'm developing math concepts and motor skills. I'm also learning how to share and work with my friends. I may use these skills as an architect or builder when I grow up.

Dramatic Play When I pretend and play dress-up, I'm learning how to be a mommy, daddy, doctor, teacher, or police officer. Dramatic play also fosters my language and social skills.

Art The art center gives me the opportunity to develop my creativity and express myself. As I experiment and have fun, I'm also developing social skills and small muscles.

Manipulatives When I play with puzzles and manipulative materials, I'm developing eye-hand coordination and learning to complete tasks.

Science I can observe, experiment, predict, and discover new things in the science area. These are the same things real scientists do.

Math The math center develops my problem-solving skills and gives me hands-on experiences in counting, comparing, patterning, and measuring. I may use these skills as an accountant or computer specialist when I grow up.

Library In the library I'm learning to love books and I'm practicing my reading skills.

Writing The writing center has lots of interesting materials so I can learn how to write stories, letters, books, and more. Maybe I'll be an author when I grow up.

Sensory Play The sensory play center allows me to use my senses in different ways. I can play in the sand or water using many different tools!

Thinking Station In the thinking station, I can do activities that help me think about things in new and different ways.

Music As I play instruments and sing, I'm expressing myself and developing listening and language skills. Music just makes me feel good!

Large Motor Center I get to move my body in the large motor center! I can use my energy to get stronger and stay in shape!

Computers I can use computers to learn many different things. I can write stories, do research, play math games, watch educational videos, and much more.

Surprise Center The activities in this center are always a surprise! I can try activities that are related to things I'm learning about at school. I can also do activities about things that interest me.

I am working, playing, and discovering in my own way in learning centers each day!

 **Reproducible Page**

Around the Room with Multicultural Ideas

A multicultural curriculum is one that represents people of all ethnic groups, ages, genders, and abilities in meaningful ways. These are some exciting ideas for implementing the anti-bias curriculum in learning centers.

Dramatic Play   Use food containers and utensils for different ethnic foods; multiethnic dolls; clothes, shoes, hats, and jewelry from a variety of cultures; full-length mirrors.

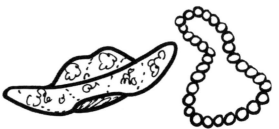

Library   Include folk tales from different cultures; books representative of our society; printed materials in different languages.

Manipulatives   Provide puzzles that do not show gender bias; graduated stacking dolls from another culture; coins and beads from other countries.

Art   Offer children crayons, markers, paint, and clay in various body colors; art media of other cultures (e.g., cloth, rice paper); pictures of art from different areas of the world.

Music   Play songs from around the world; use ethnic instruments.

Blocks/Construction   Show pictures of different kinds of homes (mobile homes, apartments, single-family dwellings; rural, suburban, urban; houses from other countries); multiethnic figures; different types of transportation; a variety of building materials, such as straw, sticks, canvas.

Sensory Play   Give children figures of animals from different habitats (arctic, rainforest, desert, forest) to play with in sand and water.

Math   Make graphs that compare families; manipulatives from different cultures; counting books in different languages.

Pictures   Throughout the room, display pictures of different families and ethnic groups; pictures that reflect diversity; men and women in different roles; children with varying abilities; pictures of children in the room and their families.

Blocks/Construction Center

Blocks help children develop concepts of number, size, shape, space, and weight. They also encourage imagination, language, social skills, self-confidence, and motor skills. Further, blocks give children a great deal of personal satisfaction and pleasure.

Materials

unit blocks – various shapes
   and sizes
shelf
carpeted floor
cardboard boxes
alphabet blocks
wooden dollhouse and furniture
wooden barn and animals
plastic dinosaurs and zoo animals
toy train set, boats, airplanes
small dolls or action figures
plastic bins or boxes for accessories
foam blocks
wooden cars and trucks

toy street signs
Lincoln Logs
bristle blocks
hollow blocks
construction hats
carpenter's apron
blueprints
paper, pencils
maps
tile or carpet samples
pattern blocks

Teacher Tips

Place blocks on a carpeted area away from quiet areas, such as the library or writing center.

Enclose the blocks/construction area on three sides with cabinets or shelves.

Provide enough space in the blocks/construction center so several children can move around and build on the floor.

Limit the number of children who can play in the area at one time.

Trace around the shapes of different unit blocks on dark construction paper and cut out the tracings. Cover these shapes with clear contact paper and tape them to shelves to help children with clean-up time.

Group like props in tubs, pails, or baskets and label with the words and pictures.

Use a large leaf basket to store blocks and have the children put all the blocks in it when they pick up.

Assign one child each day to be "block chairperson" and be responsible for cleaning up the blocks/construction center.

If children have worked hard on a structure or are not finished, allow them to leave it with a sign that says, "Please do not disturb." You can also designate a shelf as the "block gallery" where children can save their creations, or take photographs of what the children build.

Post simple rules in the block area.

Build only as tall as you are.

Only knock down what you build.

Put the blocks away when you're finished.

Block Props

Idea Box Make an idea box with pictures of different things children can build, such as a bridge, library, park, or machine.

Themes Relate blocks to stories or themes. For example, children could build a castle for Cinderella, a space station, or a model of your community.

Floor Map Involve the children in designing a floor map by drawing with markers on a piece of foam board. (Floor maps can also be made by gluing felt scraps on a large piece of felt fabric.)

Measurement Have the children use blocks to measure different objects in the classroom. For example, challenge them to find out how many blocks tall a table is, how many blocks long the room is, or how many blocks tall different friends are.

STEP IT UP Have children use rulers to measure the height and width of the structures they build. Include a balance scale in the blocks area so children can compare the weights of things they build from smaller blocks.

Computer Center

Computers are a common part of most children's everyday lives. They see their parents and older siblings using computers at home. Children should have opportunities to use computers for activities that reinforce, review, and extend the concepts they are learning in the classroom.

Children may use computers to read, write, and illustrate fiction and nonfiction, to take tests, to practice math, to watch science videos, etc. The opportunities for learning are endless!

Materials
computer

educational software

printer

scanner

digital camera

printer paper

Teacher Tips

Place the computer center in a quieter area of the classroom, such as near the library or the writing center.

Post some simple rules for computer use in the computer center. Rules may include:

▶ No food/drinks near computer

▶ Use only approved websites

▶ Use the computer carefully

▶ Ask the teacher when you need help

Limit the number of children who can use the computer at one time. Some activities/games may allow for two children, but most activities will be independent.

Adjust the computer settings so children cannot accidentally go to inappropriate websites. Most Internet programs have "parental controls" for this purpose. Your school may have additional requirements.

Have CDs, flash drives, or other devices readily available for saving children's work.

Reserve some computer-related items for teacher use only, such as the scanner and digital camera.

Dramatic Play Center

In the dramatic play area children have the opportunity to role-play real-life situations, release emotions, practice language, develop social skills, and express themselves creatively.

Materials
pretend kitchen equipment made from wood or plastic (stove, refrigerator, sink, microwave)
pots, pans, dishes, ethnic cooking utensils (chopsticks, mocahete)
dress-up clothes (children's, men's, ladies')
night clothes (robes, gowns, slippers, pajamas)
pocketbooks, hats, clip-on ties
shoes (boots, sports shoes, children's, adults', etc.)
full-length mirror
table and chairs
dolls and doll clothes (multiethnic dolls of both genders)
stuffed animals
puppets
doll bed, blankets, pillows

baby carriage
toy ironing board and iron
empty food boxes and containers
telephones
old jewelry, jewelry box
broom, mop, carpet sweeper
books and magazines
paper, pencils, grocery lists
tablecloth, plastic flowers for the table
old camera
suitcase, briefcase, billfold, keys
costumes
vests

Teacher Tips

Place the dramatic play center in a corner or define it with shelves so it is cozy.

Limit the number of children who can play in the center at a particular time.

Provide enough props to interest the children, but rotate materials so the center doesn't become cluttered and overwhelm them.

Use a clothes rack, pegboard, or plastic hooks with adhesive backs for hanging bags and clothes.

Laundry baskets can also be used for storing clothes and hats.

Cut out shapes of dishes and pans from contact paper and tape them on shelves to help children with clean-up time.

Knot long handles on bags and purses so children won't choke themselves. Cut off old clothes if they are too long so the children won't trip.

Housekeeping Props

Decorations Make the dramatic play center homey with a rug, pictures, and curtains on the window.

Windows Add a window by attaching a mirror or landscape picture to a wall. Tape on construction paper strips to look like a window frame, then add fabric or wallpaper cut like a curtain.

Washer and Dryer Cut a circle out of the front of a corrugated cardboard box. Cut a door around it and add a pipe cleaner handle. Draw knobs, dials, and details on it to make it look like a washer or dryer.

Pantyhose Hair Take an old pair of pantyhose and cut off the feet. Cut each leg into three strips and braid. Tie off the ends of each braid with a ribbon, then wear on the head like a wig.

Food Glue pictures of food in pie pans or frozen dinner trays. You can also glue labels from cans of food to toilet paper rolls to make canned goods.

Placemats Cut old plastic placemats in half for the dramatic play center. To make napkins, cut 12" squares from fabric. Napkin rings can be made by cutting 1" rings off of cardboard rollers and coloring them with markers.

Character Headbands Cut animal ears out of felt and glue them onto plastic headbands. Make pink pig ears, black cat ears, floppy brown ears for a dog, etc.

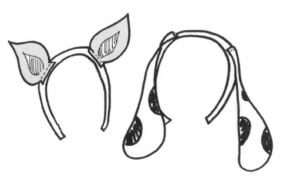

Make-Up Take old make-up (blush, powder, etc.) and pop out the contents with a knife. Cut colored felt and glue in place of the make-up. Store in an old make-up case with clean applicators and brushes. Empty a nail polish bottle. Clean the brush with remover and allow the remainder of the polish to evaporate. Fill with water so children can "paint" their nails.

Earrings   String beads on thin ribbon cut 7" long. Tie ends to make loops that children can hang on their ears.

Baby Bed   Use an old infant carrier or car seat as a baby bed in the housekeeping area. Children will also enjoy playing with old diaper bags, blankets, toys, bottles, clothes, and other baby accessories.

Pets   Add stuffed animal dogs and cats, pet bowls, dried dog biscuits, etc.

Phones   Recycle broken phones in the dramatic play area. (Wall phones are especially fun.) Make a cellular phone by covering a small box with black paper or aluminum foil. Write numerals on the phone with a marker.

Laptop Computer   Use a sturdy three-ring binder to make a pretend laptop. On the inner front cover, use construction paper to make a "screen." On the inner back cover, use construction paper to make a keyboard. Cover both with clear contact paper.

Babies   Cut a piece of flannel in a 20" to 30" square. Make a ball of polyester filling and place it in the middle of the square (back side). Wrap a rubber band around the filling to make a head. Tie ribbons around two ends to make arms. Decorate a face with fabric pens, or sew on button eyes and features. Add yarn hair if you wish.

Prop Boxes

Vary the dramatic play area with prop boxes that relate to different units of study, reflect children's interests, or extend a shared experience. All you need is a box or plastic tub for storage and some of the materials below. (A note to parents about an upcoming theme is a great way to get items for prop boxes.) These boxes can also be shared by different classrooms in the school.

Grocery Store
Empty food boxes and cans, grocery sacks, grocery cart or wagon, shelves, cash register, play money, cardboard boxes, paper and pencils, dress-up clothes, purses, billfolds (Set up a fruit stand, bakery, etc.)

Post Office
Envelopes, paper, pencils and pens, rubber stamps, stamp pad, stickers, partitioned box, cash register, play money, bag or sack for carrying mail, old hat, wagon for mail truck

Pet Shop
Stuffed animals, puppets, cardboard boxes for cages, plastic bowls, brush, towel, grooming supplies, cash register, pet toys

Restaurant
Paper plates, napkins, plastic cups, silverware, tray, notepad, pencils, apron, chef's hat, menus, cash register, play food, food pictures glued onto paper plates, telephone, carry-out food containers (Change it to be a pizza parlor, ice cream shop, or school cafeteria.)

Flower Shop
Plastic pots, artificial flowers, gloves, seed catalogs, baskets, watering can, play garden tools, phone, notepad, cash register

Doctor's Office/Hospital
Stethoscope, tongue depressors, cotton, adhesive bandages, eye chart, scale, dolls, notepad and pencils, wagon for ambulance, phone, scrub suit and mask

School
Desk for teacher, bell, calendar, paper, crayons, pencils, books, chairs, dress-up clothes, eyeglass frames, board, flag, clock

Photo Studio
Old camera, pictures, photo album, video camera (made from a small box), phone, appointment book, paper and pencils

Hat Shop/Shoe Store Old shoes (men's, women's, babies', children's, etc.), hats (make in art), purses, accessories, socks, mirror, cash register, play money, hat rack, shoe shine kit

Travel Agency Travel posters, brochures, pamphlets, books on other countries, tickets, desk, chairs, phone, calendar, notepad and pencils, souvenirs from other countries, dress-up clothes, computer

Construction Site Blueprints, hammer, nails, wood scraps, tape measure, paintbrushes, hard hat, lunch box, safety glasses, carpenter's apron, gloves, toy trucks, blocks, cardboard boxes, cell phone

Theater Tickets, cash register, chairs, empty food boxes and cups for refreshments, dress-up clothes, puppets, puppet theater, old costumes, mirror, jewelry, hats, glasses, masks

Campsite Sleeping bag, backpack, canteen, stones and sticks for fire, blanket to make a tent, play fishing pole

Airport/Train Station Phone, tickets, cash register, play money, paper and pencils, travel brochures, suitcase, dress-up clothes, chairs, food trays and paper goods, cardboard boxes to make a train

Office Computer, cash register, calculator, paper, pencils, envelopes, phone, calendar, dress-up clothes (adapt to make a bank, newspaper office, etc.)

Fire or Police Station Paper badges, whistle, helmet or hat, phone, flashlight, paper and pencils, riding toys, ticket book, map, piece of hose, boots, air tank made from empty plastic liter bottles

Filling Station Old hose, cash register, credit cards (cut-up foam trays), cars and trucks, phone, empty food packages, towel, empty spray bottle, riding toys

Party Invitations, party plates, cups, napkins, hats, favors, goodie bags, wrapping paper, tape, ribbon, empty boxes, greeting cards

Variation An art shop, circus, boat, space station, costume shop, wedding, sports store, toy shop, library, music store, and TV station are other enjoyable subjects for prop boxes.

Art Center

When you set up an open art center in your classroom, children will have the opportunity to plan and create in their own unique ways. They will be able to make choices, experiment, solve problems, and be truly creative. Provide children with a wide variety of materials that they can get out and clean up independently. (Vary the number of materials to fit the age and abilities of the children.)

Materials

shelves
easel
tables and chairs
drying rack
body-colored paints, crayons, markers
brushes
hole punch
paper (scrap, construction, cardboard)
scissors
crayons
paper sacks
paper cups
newspaper

glue, glue sticks
paper plates
tissue paper
material scraps
buttons
stapler
junk scraps (toilet paper rolls, egg cartons)
tape
cotton
magazines, catalogs
yarn
fingerpaint
wallpaper book
chalk

brads
paper clips
clay
play dough
craft sticks
foil
watercolors
pipe cleaners
colored pencils
natural objects (leaves, sticks, rocks)
prints or postcards of famous artwork

Teacher Tips

Place the art center near a sink on a washable floor. It should also be out of the flow of traffic.

Have sponges, paper towels, and a trash can handy so the children can clean up their own messes.

Use old adult shirts for smocks.

Cover the table and floor with newspaper for easy clean-up of messy projects.

Put out a few materials at a time for younger children. (They are overwhelmed if they have too many choices.)

Take time to show the children how to use and care for different materials. For example, show them how to use "just one dot of glue" or how to "put the paintbrush back in the same color."

Artful Hints

▶ Store materials in clear containers, detergent boxes with handles, large zipper bags, or tubs. Label containers with words and pictures.

▶ Ice cream barrels and plastic crates can also be used for storage bins.

▶ Plastic juice cans, margarine tubs, large plastic cups, or plastic bottoms from 2-liter drink bottles are all useful for storing markers, crayons, and chalk.

▶ Use plastic bottle caps to hold glue. Give children coffee stirrers or cotton swabs to apply the glue.

▶ To make a scissors rack, turn an egg carton upside down. Poke holes in the bottom of each section and insert scissor points in the holes.

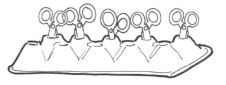

▶ Use a desk organizer for storing paper.

▶ To help children care for markers, mix plaster of Paris in a pie pan (¾" thick). Turn markers upside down with the tips of the markers in the plaster of Paris. Dry. Children can use markers, then stick them back in the tips. Dry markers can easily be replaced with new ones.

▶ Reduce paper costs by painting on newspaper, cardboard boxes, or grocery sacks.

▶ Offer children paper of different sizes, shapes, and textures.

▶ Vary interest at the easel by rotating watercolors, markers, chalk, or crayons with tempera paint.

▶ Purchase inexpensive household paintbrushes of varying widths to give children the opportunity to experiment with different sizes.

▶ Let the children do "pair painting," in which two children at a time paint a picture together.

▶ In Progress—Have a special shelf or table where children can keep unfinished projects they would like to continue working on.

See "Celebrating Children's Art" (page 83) for more creative art experiences.

Manipulatives

As children play with table toys, they develop small muscles, eye-hand coordination, attention span, social skills, and language. They also build concepts about size, shape, color, and patterns.

Materials

table and chairs	hole punch
puzzles	play dough and props
beads	parquetry blocks
sewing cards	paper and pencils
pegboard	clay
dressing toys	snap toys
stacking toys	shelves
nuts and bolts	board games
scissors	
pattern cards	
playing cards	
puzzle rack	
lacing activities	
nesting toys	
locks and keys	
take-apart toys	

Teacher Tips

Store materials in clear containers, baskets, tubs, boxes, or plastic bags at the children's eye level. Recycled ice cream buckets, detergent boxes, or cut-down plastic milk jugs can also be used.

Use pictures from the boxes the toys come in to label the shelves.

Group like objects together.

Rotate manipulatives so the shelves don't look cluttered. Children should have from 10 to 15 activities to choose from at a time.

Discard manipulatives with missing pieces or broken parts. Clean plastic toys frequently.

Manipulative Activities

Puzzles Make your own puzzles with cereal and food boxes. Cut off the front of each box and cut it into puzzle shapes. (Vary the number of puzzle pieces according to the ability of the children.)

Craft Stick Puzzles Tape eight large craft sticks together. Turn them over and draw a picture with magic markers on the sticks. Remove the tape, mix up the sticks, and ask the children to put them back together.

Stencils Cut shapes out of food boxes and plastic lids to make stencils and templates. Children will also enjoy tracing around puzzle pieces, cookie cutters, cans, and other common objects.

Floor Puzzle Make a large floor puzzle from poster board or corrugated cardboard.

Match Ups Collect plastic containers and lids from mayonnaise, soft drinks, syrup, and other foods. Children can match the containers with the lids, and screw the lids onto the containers.

Inserting Cut a slit in the lid of a potato chip canister. Give the children poker chips and ask them to put them in the hole. Children can also insert pom poms in the mouth of a milk jug.

Sewing Cards Punch holes in food boxes or paper plates, then give children shoelaces or cord so they can sew around them. Old plastic placemats can also be used to make lacing cards.

Pick Up Give children chopsticks, tweezers, or tongs and challenge them to pick up different objects, such as small toys, cotton balls, rocks, or leaves.

Stringing Let children string pasta with holes, cut-up straws, buttons, or cereal with holes on yarn or string to make a necklace. (Wrap a piece of tape around the end of the yarn so it is easier to thread the objects.)

...ugh

> ## RECIPE FOR HOMEMADE PLAY DOUGH:
>
> 2 cups all purpose flour
>
> 1 cup salt
>
> 2 tb. cream of tartar
>
> 2 tb. vegetable oil
>
> 2 cups water
>
> food coloring

Directions Mix all the ingredients together in a pan and stir until smooth. Cook over medium heat until the mixture forms a ball and sticks to the spoon. Cool and knead. Store in plastic bags or covered containers.

To make play dough that is body-colored, simply follow the directions above, omitting the food coloring. After the mixture has cooked, divide the dough into four balls. Add a different spice (such as cinnamon, chili powder, cocoa, curry, or paprika) to each ball and squeeze to mix. (Make sure there are no children with allergies to these spices before using them.) Give the children wiggly eyes and pipe cleaners to make people.

Have the children play with dough and clay on old placemats. Add scissors, cookie cutters, play dishes, birthday candles, and other cooking props.

Flubber

Flubber feels good, gooey, and fun!

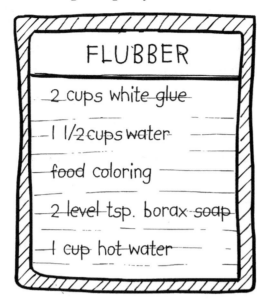

FLUBBER

2 cups white glue

1 1/2 cups water

food coloring

2 level tsp. borax soap

1 cup hot water

Directions   Combine the glue, 1½ cups water, and food coloring. In a large bowl dissolve the borax in the hot water. Slowly stir the glue mixture into the borax. It will coagulate and be difficult to mix. Pour off the excess water, then let it sit for several minutes. Drain off the remaining water. Store flubber covered in the refrigerator when it is not being used.

Goop

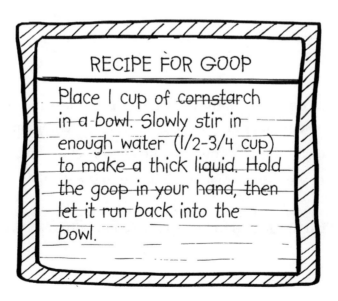

RECIPE FOR GOOP

Place 1 cup of cornstarch in a bowl. Slowly stir in enough water (1/2-3/4 cup) to make a thick liquid. Hold the goop in your hand, then let it run back into the bowl.

How is goop like a liquid? How is it like a solid?

Remind the children to always wash their hands before and after playing with play dough, flubber, or goop.

Science Center

In the science center children are able to explore, solve problems, make decisions, develop concepts about science and nature, improve language, interact socially, and develop sensory skills. Children's curiosity about the world and their interest in natural phenomena are also extended.

Materials
shelves, tables
magnifying glass
magnets
plants
prism
aquarium
balance scale
experiments
science books, magazines
pictures and posters
thermometer
flashlight
feely box
terrarium

sensory activities
models (dinosaurs, insects)
mirror
seeds, leaves, flowers, feathers
exhibits (nature collections of rocks, shells, bones, butterflies, etc.)
field guide books
clipboard, paper, pencils
planting area to grow sprouts, flowers, herbs, etc.

Teacher Tips

Arrange the science center in a quiet area of the classroom so individual or small groups of children can explore. (A window nearby is helpful for growing plants or for watching the world.)

Organize the materials in baskets, in tubs, or on trays. Rotate collections frequently to spark new interest.

Label the objects in the science area. Encourage the children to use the field guides, books, posters, and magazines for research.

Encourage the children and parents to add to the science center with objects they find in their yards or on trips.

Place fragile specimens in zipper bags or clear deli containers so the children can investigate them with a magnifying glass.

Create generic investigation sheets that children can use to design their own investigations, record observations, and record their conclusions.

Super Science Ideas

Color Paddles Color paddles can be made with paper plates and red, yellow, and blue acetate (clear report folders work well). Cut circles out of the acetate the size of the plates. Cut the centers out of six plates. Take the red acetate and staple it between two paper plates. Do the same for the blue and yellow. The children can hold up the plates and experiment with making the secondary colors.

Sounds Like Take ten empty paper bags. Put rice in two of the bags, popcorn kernels in two, paper clips in two, salt in two, and pennies in two. Glue the bags closed and mix them up. Let the children try to find the ones that sound alike when shaken.

Sniff and Tell Put items with distinct smells (bubble gum, cocoa, cinnamon sticks, coffee grounds, baby powder) in the bottoms of different paper bags. Glue the bags closed, then poke several holes in the top. Children can smell each bag and try to identify the odor.

New Pennies Mix a cup of vinegar with 2 tb. of salt. Let the children take old pennies and stir them in this solution to make "shiny new pennies."

Volcano! Fill a pie pan with sand. Put a bottle in the middle and build up around it with the sand. Pour ½ cup vinegar in the bottle and add several drops of red food coloring. Add 2 tb. of baking soda to the vinegar and look out!

Mirror Magic Cut small pictures from magazines or catalogs in half and glue one half of each picture onto a file folder. The children can take a small hand mirror and put it next to the picture to make the other half.

Research and Read Collect leaves from different trees on the playground. Give the children a field guide book of trees and challenge them to identify the leaves by matching them up with pictures in the book. (Children can do similar activities with shell and rock collections.) Have children classify the leaves according to their features and the kinds of trees they come from.

Hairy Plants Draw a face on a plain paper cup. Fill the cup with dirt and sprinkle grass seed on top. Water and place in the sun. When the "hair" (grass) gets long, give it a haircut with scissors.

Discovery Bottles

*Use plastic drink bottles to make these "hands-on" discovery bottles for your science center. ***

Muddy Bottle — Put ½ cup dirt in the bottom of a bottle, and fill the bottle with water. Let the children shake it up and watch the dirt settle. (Try using gravel, peat moss, clay, and different types of soil.)

Collect soil samples from different states or countries and make muddy bottles from them. Label the bottles so the children can compare the soil found in different areas.

Wave Bottle — Fill the bottle ⅔ full with water. Add several drops of food coloring to the water, then fill it to the top with vegetable oil. Turn the bottle on its side and move it back and forth to make waves.

Magnet Bottle — Fill the bottle half full with sand or salt. Add pins, paper clips, and small metallic objects to the sand and shake. Let the children take a magnet and try to find the hidden objects.

Bubble Bottle — Add 1 cup of water, a squirt of dish detergent, and 2 drops of food coloring to the bottle. Shake to make bubbles.

Sound Bottle — Put beans, popcorn kernels, and rice in different bottles. Stick each bottle inside an old sock. Let the children shake and guess what's in the bottles.

Density Bottle — Take three bottles. Fill one with water, one with vegetable oil, and one with clear shampoo. Add a marble to each bottle, then screw on the lids. The children can observe how the marbles move through different liquids.

* Secure the lids of these bottles with a glue gun or super glue.

Stress Bottle Pour ⅓ cup clear corn syrup in a bottle. Add glitter, sequins, or small toys. The children can hold the bottle and slowly turn it around. This will help them focus and relax.

Color Bottle Add red food coloring and water to a bottle and label it with the word "red." Make a different color bottle to add to the science center every day.

Seasonal Bottle Put autumn leaves, flowers, or other natural objects in bottles of water. The children can observe the objects as they disintegrate. (Silk flowers and leaves can also be used.)

Hidden Objects Bottle Fill a bottle ⅔ full with sand or salt. Add five to ten small objects to the bottle and shake it. Challenge the children to find all of the hidden objects.

Glitter Bottles Add glitter, confetti, or crayon shavings to bottles of water.

Seriation Bottles Take four or five bottles and put a different amount of water in each one, from empty to full. Mix the bottles up, then let the children seriate them from empty to full.

Squishy Bags

Plastic bags give children the opportunity to observe and investigate a variety of materials and objects.

Materials
- ☐ plastic zipper bags
- ☐ shaving cream
- ☐ food coloring
- ☐ bubble solution
- ☐ dirt
- ☐ natural objects, such as shells, bones, flowers, leaves, etc.
- ☐ magnifying glass

Color Bags Squirt shaving cream into a bag. Add a drop of red and a drop of yellow food coloring. Zip shut. Let the children squeeze the bag to make orange. (Add red and blue to another bag, and yellow and blue to a third bag.)

Bubble Bag Pour a little commercial or homemade bubble solution in a baggie and let the children squeeze and shake it up.

Muddy Bag Put dirt in a baggie and add a little water. Play in the mud without getting dirty.

Investigation Bag Place shells, rocks, sand, leaves, or other natural objects children can explore in plastic zipper bags. Give them a magnifying glass to enlarge specimens.

th Center

Children will have opportunities to count, group, make patterns, tell time, measure, explore shapes, make comparisons, and join and separate sets in the math center. Small motor skills, problem-solving, and social skills will also be developed.

Materials

shelves, table
toy clock
calculator
play money
rulers
tape measure
craft sticks
small toys
geometric shapes
tactile numerals and shapes
puzzles
measuring cups and spoons
Cuisenaire™ rods
counting cubes
dominoes
dice
deck of cards
geoboard
attribute blocks
paper and pencils
dry-erase board
computer
play phone

stopwatch, minute timer
number line
pattern blocks
file folder games
bathroom scale
sorting tray or box
balance scale
coins (American and foreign)
objects to count (shells, rocks, buttons, toothpicks, keys, bottle caps, pasta, nuts and bolts, paint chips, etc.)

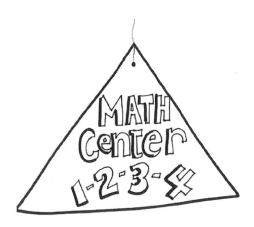

Teacher Tips

Label baskets, tubs, and clear containers where math manipulatives are stored.

Make math games that integrate themes and concepts you are studying. (Play these as a large group activity, then place them in the math center to encourage small groups of children to play.)

Meaningful Math

Addition and Subtraction
Give children muffin papers and cereal or pretzels to use in working out math problems. (Of course, it's fun to eat them when they're finished.)

One-to-One
Have children practice one-to-one correspondence by placing objects in egg cartons, muffin pans, and other separated containers.

Make paper placemats with outlines of dishes and silverware for the children to match up.

Sorting
Use a silverware tray or divided relish dish for sorting activities. In addition, paper sacks, plastic berry baskets, shoe boxes, or paper plates can be used for sorting. Large objects can be sorted into hula hoops.

Counting
Dye pasta to use as math counters. Separate into four plastic bags. Add 1 tb. rubbing alcohol and a large squirt of food coloring to each bag. Shake. Dry on wax paper.

Birthday candles, party favors, hair bows, leaves, plastic cutlery, blocks, coupons, crayons, and other common classroom objects can also be used for counting and sorting activities.

Small, inexpensive toys can make interesting manipulatives for math.

Patterns
Make pattern cards by gluing colored toothpicks or pasta onto sentence strips. The children can then reproduce the patterns using the real objects. Have children make additional pattern cards for their classmates to reproduce.

Seriation
To make a seriation game, cut cardboard rolls from wrapping paper or paper towels into different lengths.

Place Value
Draw a line down the middle of a file folder. Write "tens" on the left side and "ones" on the right. Have the children make sets of ten out of craft sticks and rubber bands. Children can use bundles of ten and individual sticks to tell place value.

Math Activities

There are many fun ways for children to learn new math skills and to reinforce skills they already have.

Foursquare — Use chalk to draw a large square on the concrete and divide it into four smaller squares. Have one child stand in each square. Have children bounce a ball to each other and count by 2s, 5s, and 10s as they bounce the ball.

Measurement Tools — Put out a variety of classroom objects on a table, some small and some large. Give children rulers and yardsticks and encourage them to choose the best tool to measure each object. Have each child work with a partner to measure the items.

I Spy — Play "I Spy" to reinforce knowledge of geometric figures. For example, you could say "I spy with my little eye a hexagon." Children would need to find a figure with six sides in the classroom.

Hundreds Chart

Materials — ☐ large poster of hundreds chart, large sticky notes, paper, pencil

Directions — Display the hundreds chart at eye level for children. Before children come into class, put sticky notes over specific numbers on the chart (all of the tens, for example). Have children study the hundreds chart and write the numbers they think are covered without peeking. As a class, pull off the sticky notes to reveal the hidden numbers.

Variation — Have one child use sticky notes to cover numbers in a pattern on the chart, and have the rest of the class guess what the pattern is.

Outdoor Math   Let children bring rulers, yardsticks, and balance scales outside. Have children choose objects found in nature and measure their weight and length. Have children record their measurements and share them with the class.

Shape Building   Give children pattern blocks. Have children experiment with putting the blocks together to make new shapes. For example, they can put two triangles together to make a rectangle.

Pattern Path   Cut large shapes from pieces of felt. Start a pattern path on the floor with the shapes. Have a child walk on the pattern path and name each shape as he steps on it. Have children choose the shape that should come next in the pattern.

Library

The library should be inviting and interesting, and a place where children fall in love with books. In the library area, children can also develop oral language, listening skills, and reading readiness skills while they learn new concepts.

Materials
books (all sizes, shapes, subjects)
comfortable seating (pillows,
    bean bag chairs, small rocking
    chairs, etc.)
book rack and shelves
Big Books
magazines
travel brochures
flannel board and stories
puppets
catalogs
sensory books
maps
picture books
menus
dictionary
letters
pictures and posters
class-made books

listening station
calendars
CDs
multilingual children's books
poems or language experience stories
newspapers and magazines in
    different languages and print

Teacher Tips

Check out books from your public library to add to your classroom.

Encourage parents to donate books and magazines their children no longer use.

Rather than a holiday gift, request that parents donate a book to your classroom.

Yard sales and thrift stores are good sources for inexpensive books.

Model how to open books, turn pages, and care for them. When books are torn up, involve the children in repairing them.

Let the children help you categorize the books. You might have sections for animal stories, folk tales, nature books, Big Books, etc. Ask the children to draw pictures to use as labels.

Liven Up the Library!

Loft   Build a reading loft for the library area. Store books underneath and place pillows on top.

Book Buddies   Add "book buddies" (stuffed animals) children can read to.

Reading Lamp   Add a small table and a lamp the children can turn on when they want to read.

Reading Pool   To make a reading pool where children will want to take a dip, fill a plastic swimming pool with books, pillows, and a quilt.

Tent   Make a tent in the library with a sleeping bag, flashlight, and books.

Book Nook   Decorate an appliance box to use as a reading nook.

Puppets   Make puppets of favorite characters from books so the children can create their own stories in the library.

Author's Basket   Add an Author's Basket to your library area. Put all of the books you have by a particular author in the basket. Add a label with the author's name and perhaps a photograph.

Magazine Rack   Magazine racks are handy for storing printed materials. Ask a grocery store manager to save an old rack or a promotional display you can use.

Tub Time   Paint an old bathtub and fill it with pillows and books.

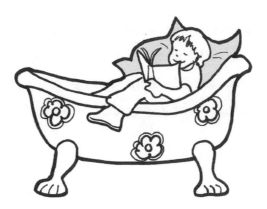

Writing Center

Emergent literacy will flourish in a writing center. Children will develop a positive attitude about school as they work on their reading, writing, vocabulary, social, listening, and small motor skills.

Materials

table and chairs
pens, pencils, crayons, markers
variety of paper (colored, notepads, different shapes and sizes)
tissue paper
envelopes
blank books (fold 2 pieces of paper in half and staple)
sticky notes
junk mail
bank deposit slips, magazine inserts, book order forms
chalkboard and chalk
wipe-off board and dry-erase markers
magic slate
stamps and ink pad
scissors, hole punch
glue, tape, stapler

computer and printer
picture file
picture dictionary
magnetic letters
clipboard
used postcards or greeting cards
reading games

Teacher Tips

Store writing materials in a shoe rack or desk organizer.

Rotate the paper and materials in the writing center to increase children's interest.

Save samples of what the children do in the writing center to add to their portfolios.

Include opportunities to write using a computer on a regular basis.

Write On

Class Directory Make a class directory so the children can write to their friends. Print each child's name on an index card and glue on his or her picture. Store the cards in a small box, or punch holes in the cards and hang on a metal ring.

Writer's Wall Create a Writer's Wall of Fame near the writing center to display children's work.

Word Bank Children can use a word bank like a "spell check" to look up words they want to write. You will need a 3" × 5" file box with an alphabetical index. Print sight words, vocabulary words, spelling words, and other words children request on index cards and file them in the box alphabetically.

Sand Tray Make a sand tray children can use to practice writing letters and words. Glue colorful construction paper in the bottom of a shirt box, then sprinkle one to two cups of sand or salt over the bottom of the box. Children can trace the letters in the box with their fingers for tactile learning.

School Days Add an old school desk to the writing center so the children can play school.

Computer Writing Include a computer in the writing center. Have children type and illustrate poems and stories on the computer. Older children can write reports and create slideshows that include pictures and video.

Sensory Play

Sand and water experiences give children sensory pleasure while developing math concepts, small motor skills, social skills, and language.

Materials
sand or water table (You can also use your classroom sink, plastic tubs, or a wading pool.)
spoons, shovels, pots, pails, watering can
smocks
toy dishes
plastic containers
bottles
measuring cups
plastic graduated cylinders
funnels
sponges
washable baby dolls, clothes
sifter, strainer

plastic boats, ping-pong balls
towel
water wheel
piece of hose, clear tubing
plastic cars and trucks
plastic animals, toys
beaters, eye droppers

Teacher Tips

Sensory play should be located on washable flooring near a sink. A bath mat, shower curtain, or drop cloth can also be used to cover the floor.

A hand vacuum cleaner is handy for cleaning up spilled sand or rice. Sponges, mops, and towels will also enable children to clean up after themselves.*

Provide smocks for the children to wear when playing in water.

Give children simple rules, such as, "Keep the sand and water in the tub," or "If you spill something, clean it up."

Limit the number of children who can play in the area at one time. Cut feet shapes from colored contact paper and stick them on the floor to indicate the number of children who can play.

Move the sand and water table outside onto the playground in warm weather.

Remind children to wash their hands before and after playing with sensory materials.

* Tell children that the hand vacuum should never be used anywhere near water. It is only to be used to pick up dry items.

"Sensational" Activities

Creative Materials For different sensory experiences, use birdseed, rice, dried beans, cornmeal, oatmeal, paper confetti, pasta (cooked or raw), cotton balls, dirt, shaving cream, foam peanuts, leaves, and other natural objects. Mix items together, such as dried beans and rice, cardboard rollers and cornmeal, or sand and seashells.

Individual Play Put plastic tubs in a wading pool on the floor. Fill the tubs with different items, and each child can sit down and play in her own space. Clear lids from deli trays are good for individual sensory play, too.

Scoop It Draw faces on ping-pong balls with a permanent marker and float them in the water table. Give children a small fishnet to scoop them up. Other plastic toys, such as counting bears, can be scooped up with a fishnet or picked up with tongs.

Smells and Colors Add soap bubbles, glitter, food coloring, or fragrances (vanilla, mint) to the water table.

Wet Sand Wet the sand for molding and building sand castles. A spray bottle of water works well for this.

Icebergs Fill large plastic containers almost to the top with colored water and freeze to make icebergs. Place the icebergs in the water table with plastic arctic animals.

Sifting Mix shells and other small objects into the sand. Give children a sieve or strainer to find them. Spray-paint pebbles gold to make "nuggets" the children can pan for.

Magnets Hide metallic objects such as paper clips and screws in the sand and let children find them with a magnet.

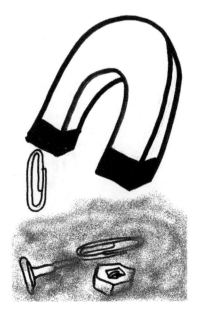

Sink and Float   Lay out a variety of different objects and ask the children to predict which ones will sink and which ones will float. Have them experiment to see if their predictions are correct.

Rainbow Rice   Make rainbow rice by mixing 2 tablespoons of rubbing alcohol and a big squirt of food coloring. Pour it into a bottle of rice and shake. Dry on wax paper. Dye different bottles of rice red, blue, yellow, and green, then mix them all together. (This rice can also be used for art projects. Make a design with glue on a sheet of paper, then sprinkle the rainbow rice on it to create a collage.)

Bubbles   Fill bowls with water and dish detergent. (Dawn™ and Joy™ work best.) Give children egg beaters so they can beat up some mountains of bubbles. Fill small cups with a mixture of dish detergent and water; give children straws with which to blow bubbles.

Bath Time   Let children wash plastic baby dolls and toys with soap and washcloths. They will also have fun washing doll clothes and hanging them up to dry.

Boats   Children will enjoy experimenting with building boats using aluminum foil, clay, polystyrene, corks, and sponges. They can glue craft sticks together to make rafts, or carve soap bars with a plastic knife to make a boat.

Mud Pies   Every child should experience the joy of making mud pies. Mix four parts dirt with one part flour. Add enough water so it can be molded like clay. Dry.

Fishing   Cut fish shapes out of sponges, foam plates, or colored acetate (plastic report covers). Attach a paper clip to each fish and float the fish in the water. Make a fishing pole to catch them by tying a piece of string to a magnet and tying the other end to a small stick.

STEP IT UP   Fill three small tubs nearly to the top with vegetable oil in one tub, water in another tub, and light corn syrup in the last tub. Have children drop the same type of object (marble, small cube, binder clip, etc.) into each tub at the same time and see which object sinks the fastest. Have children compare and contrast the buoyancy of different liquids.

Thinking Station

Critical thinking, problem-solving, and creativity will be nurtured with these open-ended tasks.

Estimating

Materials   ☐ clear jar   ☐ small objects (candy, beads, crayons, coins, etc.)
☐ paper, pencils

Directions   Fill the jar with one kind of object. Ask the children to guess how many objects are in the jar and write their answers on pieces of paper. Count the objects at the end of the day to see whose guess was closest.

Mystery Object

Materials   ☐ box with a lid
☐ interesting objects from nature, souvenirs from other countries, etc.
☐ paper, pencils

I am green.
I grow in trees.
You can make pies with me.
What am I?

Directions   Place an object in the box and tape the lid on the box. Write clues about what is in the box; have the children draw a picture or write a sentence about what they think it is.

Alike and Different

Materials   ☐ common objects such as paper clips, rubber bands, toothpicks, crayons, etc.
☐ paper, pencils

Directions   Put out two or three objects. Have the children fold a piece of paper in half. On one side of the paper they write how the objects are alike, and on the other side, how they are different.

STEP IT UP   Have children make a Venn diagram for the two objects they are comparing. Ask children to list how the objects are alike in the overlapping section of the circles, and list how the objects are different in the separate sections of the circles.

Illustration Information

Materials ☐ interesting magazine pictures or photographs
☐ paper and pencil

Directions Display one of the pictures and ask the children to imagine that it is an illustration from a story. Have children write or dictate a short story based on what they see in the picture.

Inventions

Materials ☐ recycled materials (boxes, bottle caps, polystyrene pieces, foil, cans, etc.)
☐ tape, scissors, glue, paper scraps

Directions Put out the objects and have the children make new inventions.

Brainstorm

Materials ☐ items that relate to a season or unit of study, such as a pumpkin, magnet, wheel, etc.
☐ paper, pencils

Directions Place a unique object in the thinking station and ask the children to make a list of all the different ways it could be used.

Make a pie.

beat it like a drum!

Sit on it.

Make a carriage out of it

Roll it!

Music Center

Through music children can improve auditory skills, verbal expression, motor skills, creativity, and social skills while they derive personal enjoyment.

Materials
musical instruments
ethnic instruments
homemade instruments
CD player or MP3 player
CDs
keyboard
autoharp
tone bells
xylophone
piano
musical toys
music box
radio
listening station
visuals for songs
puppets
international music
scarves, ribbon streamers
instruments from other countries
song books
sheet music

Teacher Tips

Hang rhythm instruments from hooks on the back of a shelf or a pegboard.

Model how to play the instruments so the children can make music and not noise.

Take instruments outside and have a parade.

Put a green piece of tape on the "play" button and a red piece of tape on the "stop" button to help children use the CD player independently.

Drum Beat Poetry

Children will enjoy incorporating the beat of a drum into the reading and writing of poems.

Materials
- ☐ books with favorite poems
- ☐ small drum and drumstick
- ☐ poetry CDs

Directions Read a favorite poem aloud to the class. As you read, beat the drum to the rhythm of the poem. Explain that many poems have a rhythm that makes them more interesting to listen to as they're read aloud. Choose another poem that the children know by heart. As you recite that poem together, have one child beat the drum to the rhythm of the poem. Repeat with a variety of new and familiar poems until each child has had a turn to use the drum. Put the drum in the music center. Encourage children to beat the drum to the beat of familiar poems as children recite them. Have children listen to poetry CDs and beat the drum to the rhythm as they listen.

Variations Make the drum available to children in the music center as they write their own poems. Children can beat the drum to make sure their poems have the rhythm they desire.

Have children clap their hands or stomp their feet to the rhythm of the poem.

Tin Pan Band

Drums   Make drums from oatmeal boxes, canisters, boxes, and coffee cans.

Drumsticks   Drumsticks can be made by wrapping cloth (5" circles) around cotton balls at the end of a pencil. Rubberband in place.

Guitar   Make a guitar by stretching rubber bands over the opening of a cardboard box and plucking.

Cymbals   Pie pans or paper plates can be used as cymbals to make a soft sound.

Bells   String bells on elastic and tie ends together; wear on wrists or ankles. You can also string bells to ponytail holders with twist ties.

Rhythm Sticks   Use paper towel rolls as rhythm sticks.

Shakers   Put dried beans, rice, popcorn kernels, or pasta in plastic jars, bottles, frosting cans, or small milk jugs to make shakers.

Hand Rattles   Cut a 1½" slit in a tennis ball with a knife. Squeeze the sides to open the hole, then insert beans or small pebbles. Shake for a soft sound.

Tambourines   Glue or staple two paper plates together ⅔ of the way around. Put a few beans or popcorn kernels in the middle, then staple the opening closed. Decorate with markers and crepe paper streamers.

Kazoos   Kazoos are fun to make for the whole class. Poke three holes in the side of a cardboard toilet paper roll with a pencil. Wrap wax paper over one end and rubberband in place. Hum a tune into the other end.

Sand Blocks   Glue sandpaper to blocks of wood. Hold a block in each hand and slide them back and forth against each other.

Xylophone   Cut wrapping paper rolls into different lengths and play with a wooden spoon.

Water Bells   Fill glasses or glass drink bottles with different amounts of water. Strike them with a metal spoon to create different sounds.

Rainstick   To make a rainstick, purchase a mailing tube at the post office. Let children hammer roofing nails into the tube. (Make sure the nails you use are shorter than the diameter of the mailing tube.) Fill with rice, dried beans, and aquarium gravel. Glue the lids onto the tubes. Decorate with markers, crayons, or paint. Slowly rotate the tube back and forth to make the sound of rain.

"Reading" Notes   Purchase a set of colored tone bells. Use crayons with colors that match the tone bells to make dots on the index cards so that when the appropriate bells are played, they'll produce simple songs.

STEP IT UP   Invite children to use the Internet to research how different instruments are made. Ask each child to choose a different instrument, and have them write or present a brief report about it.

Large Motor Center

(Indoor or Outdoor)

In the large motor area children develop coordination, strength, large muscles, physical fitness, and social skills; they also can release energy and frustrations.

Materials
balls (large, medium, small)
balance beam
bean bags
climbing equipment
hula hoops
tumbling mats
play gym
slide
CD player or MP3 player
parachute
jump rope
riding toys
scarves

Teacher Tips

If space is available indoors, a special area for motor activity will be enjoyed by children. This should be set up away from quiet areas so children won't disturb each other.

Limit the number of children who can play in the center at a particular time.

Give simple guidelines for using the equipment. Make rebus cards that will help the children remember the rules.

Fun and Games

Bean Bags   Make a bean bag by filling an old sock with a cup of dried beans. Wrap a rubber band around the middle of the sock, and pull the cuff of the sock over it to make a bean bag. (For younger children, fill the sock with cotton balls or foam peanuts so they won't hurt each other when they throw them.)

Tossing Box   Toss bean bags into holes cut in a box. (Children can also toss bean bags or balls into a laundry basket or trash can.)

Catch Can   Give children a potato chip canister. Let them bounce tennis balls and try to catch them in the can.

Paper Balls   Make paper balls by wadding up scrap paper and wrapping masking tape around it.

Space Ball   Cut off one leg of a pair of pantyhose at the knee. Stuff the remainder of the pantyhose in the toe of the cut-off leg and tie a knot around it. Throw it in the air and you have a space ball.

Hand Ball   Staple two paper plates together ¾" of the way around. Insert a hand in the hole and you have a paddle you can use to play handball with a paper ball.

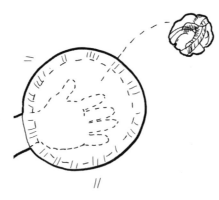

Basketball Hoop Stretch a coat hanger into a circle. Tie on 18" strips of plastic ribbon or strips cut from fabric. Bend the hook of the hanger down over a door or drawer to hang it. Use paper balls or small foam balls to toss into the hoop.

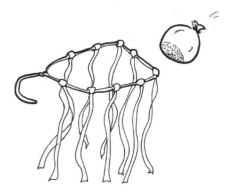

Tunnels Cut both ends off of several cardboard boxes and join the boxes together with tape. Children will enjoy crawling through this long tunnel.

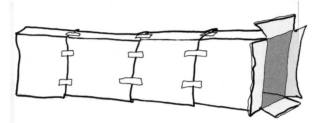

Ribbon Wands Children can make their own ribbon wands for dancing by stapling 3' pieces of ribbon or crepe paper to straws.

Silent Ball Have children sit on the floor or in chairs. Have children throw a beach ball or foam ball to each other, while remaining silent. Add a challenge to the game by having children put one hand behind their backs, close one eye, or throw with their non-dominant hand.

Balance Beam Lay a piece of 2" × 4' lumber on the floor, to make a balance beam children can walk on. Add a challenge by asking children to close their eyes.

Surprise Center

What a refreshing idea for a rotating center in your classroom! Use children's interests, classroom themes, or holidays as a springboard for this center. It should be fun, open-ended, and designed to meet the children's developmental needs. Provide enough materials to interest and challenge the children, but don't overwhelm them. (Locate the surprise center in a designated area of the classroom so children will know it's an area where there will be changes.)

Cutting Caboose

Materials
- ☐ large appliance box (large enough to hold 2 chairs)
- ☐ scissors, scrap paper, tape, file holder
- ☐ 2 small chairs
- ☐ red paint, brushes
- ☐ black construction paper
- ☐ utility knife

Directions Cut a door out of the box similar to the one illustrated. Let the children paint the box red, then cut out four black paper circles and glue them onto the box for wheels. Place two chairs in the box facing each other. Tie a pair of scissors to each chair, then tape onto the side of the box a file folder with scrap paper. The children sit in the chairs facing each other and "cut away" in the "cutting caboose."

Variation For younger children, create a "tearing train" and give them old magazines or paper they can tear into little pieces.

STEP IT UP

Have children cut out a variety of geometric figures while in the cutting caboose. They can cut out their own figures, or trace templates and cut them out. Have children name the figures they cut and label each one.

Wrapping Station

Materials ☐ gift boxes, inexpensive wrapping paper, tissue paper, funny papers, tape, scissors, ribbon, paper, pens, envelopes, old greeting cards

Directions Let the children wrap the boxes and decorate them with ribbons and cards.

Shoe Story

Materials ☐ pair of shoes, paper, pencil

Directions Display a pair of shoes. It can be any type of shoe, but the more unique, the better. Ask children to study the shoes. Children can handle the shoes if they wish. Then ask children to think about the person who might wear those shoes. Have each child describe that person. Then ask each one to write or tell a story with that person as the main character.

Variation Have children make a class list of adjectives to describe the shoes.

Joke Center

Materials ☐ riddle books, joke books, comic strips, funny pictures, paper, colored pencils

Directions After children read the riddle and joke books, they can tell some of their own jokes to a partner or draw their own comics.

STEP IT UP Have children write and illustrate their own riddles and jokes. At the end of each day, have a different child share one of their riddles or jokes with the class.

Fitness Center

Materials ☐ workout clothes, small weights, fitness DVD, TV and DVD player, health magazines, jump rope, exercise equipment

Directions Children can experiment with wearing the sports clothes and doing exercises.

Picnic Party

Materials ☐ picnic basket, tablecloth, play food, paper products, radio, sunglasses, empty bottles, and food boxes

Directions Spread out the blanket on the floor and put the basket of items on it. Have children sit on the blanket and take the objects out of the basket as they count them (up to 20). Then have children count backwards from 20 as they put the objects back in the basket.

Variations Have children count the objects by 2s, 5s, and 10s.

Have children write problems using the objects in the basket. For example, 3 spoons + 2 napkins = 5 items.

Reading Around Town

Materials ☐ books about different occupations in a neighborhood/town (firefighter, police officer, teacher, librarian, mayor, postal worker, garbage collector, newspaper/TV reporter, etc.)

Directions Have children read books about different occupations. Ask children to tell a partner what they read about that job, and if they found the job interesting.

Rain Forest

Materials ☐ books, rainsticks, stuffed animals (monkeys, birds, etc.), paper vines hanging down, CD of rain forest sounds, CD player, drums

Directions Children can visit a rain forest by exploring the objects and books.

Computer City

Materials ☐ old computer keyboards (cut cords off back), paper, pencils, play phone, calculators, calendars, computer paper

Directions Children can pretend to be in an office as they become familiar with a keyboard.

Giggles and Squiggles

Materials ☐ foam packing, foam trays, craft sticks, toothpicks, pipe cleaners, egg cartons, tape, pictures of modern art

Directions Let children create sculptures with the recycled objects.

STEP IT UP Have each child write a story about her sculpture. Invite children to display their sculptures and read their stories aloud to the class.

Holiday Happenings

Adapt the surprise center to seasons and holidays. Weave a Basket, Mask Makers, Salute to America, and Healthy Harvest are a few ideas.

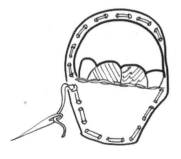   

PART 6
Game Time

A continual dilemma for teachers is how to ensure children develop necessary skills, while providing them with creative and meaningful learning opportunities.

Curriculum objectives, standards, and lists of basic skills will not go away, but these fun games will add a little more interest and challenge to the process of meeting these goals. Games are great tools for reinforcing concepts taught and for introducing new concepts in a fun and inviting way.

The games in this section can be used as choice activities in centers, with small groups of children who need additional help, or with a large group whenever you have a few extra minutes to reinforce skills.

In addition, parents could check these games out to work with their children at home, or you could plan a workshop for parents so they could construct some of their own games.

Consider these tips in making games:

▶ Keep games short and simple by focusing on one concept or skill.

▶ Make games colorful, attractive, and neat. Laminate or cover the games with clear contact paper to protect them.

▶ Try to make games in which all children will have fun and win.

▶ Adapt games to be simpler or more challenging to meet the unique needs of your students.

▶ Make self-contained games that can be stored in zipper bags, clasp envelopes, file folders, boxes, paper bags, or tubs.

▶ Demonstrate how to play the games, and then offer support until children have become familiar with the directions.

▶ Provide children with a wide variety of games for large group, small group, and individual play.

Lucky Stars

Construct this game with activities children can do if they finish their work or "can't think of anything to do."

Materials
- ☐ coffee can or oatmeal canister
- ☐ construction paper cut in star shapes
- ☐ fine-tip markers

Directions
Cut out stars from the construction paper and write one of the activities below on each star. Place the stars in the can and tell children they can choose a "lucky star" if they need something to do.

Activities
Read a book.

Write a letter to a friend.

Play a board game.

Make a gift for someone in the art area.

Work a puzzle.

Build a castle with blocks.

Play a computer math game.

Do some exercises.

Make a book.

Do a job for your teacher.

Measure the lengths of all of your pencils.

Make a pet you'd like with play dough.

Put on a puppet show.

Find a friend and draw a picture together.

Look out the window. Draw a picture of what you see.

Sing a song.

Variations
Adapt these activities to the interests and abilities of the children in your classroom.

Ask children to contribute fun ideas to the "lucky star" can.

Decorate the "lucky star" can with glitter or stickers.

Funny Ears

This self-checking game enables children to correct themselves and learn independently.

Materials
- ☐ construction paper
- ☐ bunny pattern on the following page
- ☐ scissors
- ☐ markers

Directions   Cut out 10 to 15 bunnies using the pattern on the following page. Draw a face on each and fold over its ear as shown. Write a math fact on the body of each bunny. Print the answer under its ear. Children play the game by saying the answer to the math problem, and then checking under the bunny's ear to verify their answer.

Variations   Number the bunnies; then have the children number their papers and write the answer for each question.

For younger children, put spots on the bunnies; have them count the spots and check the correct number under the bunny's ear.

Put pictures on the bunnies and ask children to identify the initial consonant sound. Write the correct letter under each bunny's ear.

Alphagories

Letters, beginning sounds, and parts of speech are all reinforced with this challenging game.

Materials
- [ ] 2 pieces of poster board (different colors)
- [ ] scissors, markers

Directions Cut each piece of poster board into twenty-four 4" squares. On one set of squares, print the letters of the alphabet. (Print "xyz" on one square.) Write the following categories on the other set of squares:

title of a book	body part
color	game or sport
famous person	something outside
television show	song title
animal	toy
something that flies	something in the school
fruit or vegetable	plant
city or town	country or state
type of transportation	action
occupation	river, lake, or ocean
machine	piece of clothing
food	restaurant or store

Tell children that you will draw a card from each pile. They have to try to think of a word that begins with the letter on one card and fits the category on the other card. After children have practiced playing the game several times, divide them into teams and play. Give the team that comes up with a response first the point. (Shuffle cards between each round to create new possibilities.)

Variation Allow small groups of children to play Alphagories and compete individually.

Boom!

Children will have fun learning new words and practicing familiar words with this game.

Materials
☐ potato chip can
☐ craft sticks
☐ construction paper
☐ scissors, glue, markers

Directions Cover a potato chip can with construction paper to look like a stick of dynamite. Write "Boom!" on the can. Write high-frequency words on craft sticks. On several other sticks, write the word "Boom!" Place the sticks in the can and shake. Children take turns passing the can around the room. If they can identify the word on the stick, they may keep it. If they select "Boom!" they must return all of their sticks to the can.

Variations Use this game to practice reading, science, and social studies vocabulary. Have children read the word and give a definition.

Have children read the word and give other words that start with the same sound or rhyme with that word.

Have children read the word and give a synonym or antonym for the word.

Have children read the word and use it in a sentence.

Muffin Man

Sing a song, play a game, and learn, all at the same time!

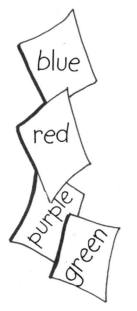

Materials ☐ different colors of construction paper

Directions Have children sit in a circle. Hold up one color at a time and sing the song below to the tune of "Do You Know the Muffin Man?"

> *Do you see the color blue,*
> *The color blue, the color blue?*
> *Do you see the color blue*
> *Somewhere in the room?*

Choose a child to point to an object that color as he or she sings back to you:

> *Yes, I see the color blue,*
> *The color blue, the color blue.*
> *Yes, I see the color blue*
> *Somewhere in the room.*

Continue holding up different colors and singing about them as children point to objects in the room.

Variation Use letters, numerals, words, or shapes in place of colors in the song and have children find them in the classroom.

Handy Signs

Children will be exposed to manual communication and how people who are hearing-impaired talk to each other with their hands.

Materials
☐ copy of the American Manual Alphabet (see following page)
☐ poster board
☐ index cards
☐ scissors, glue

Directions
Enlarge two copies of the signs on the following page on a copy machine. Glue one set onto the poster board. Cut apart the hand signs of the other set and glue them onto index cards. Shuffle up the cards and place them face down on the table. One child at a time draws a card, makes the sign with her hand, and then tries to match the sign on the index card with the one on the poster. Have children continue drawing the cards until all of the letters have been identified.

Variations
Challenge children to learn how to spell their names with signs.

Let children practice spelling words by signing them.

Teach children other signs for common phrases or songs.

Encourage children to learn how to sign a complete sentence using the sign language alphabet. Have each child sign a sentence for the class, and have the class try to figure out the sentence.

Catch a Whale by the Tail

Children will have a whale of a time learning with this game!

Materials
- ☐ cardboard roller from a pants hanger
- ☐ magnet
- ☐ construction paper, scissors
- ☐ paper clips
- ☐ string or yarn (24" long)
- ☐ markers

Directions Cut out whales from the construction paper using the pattern below. Print a different letter on each whale. Attach a paper clip to the tail of each whale. To make a fishing pole, tie one end of the string to the cardboard roller, and tie the other end of the string to the magnet. Spread the whales out on the floor. Children take turns trying to catch a whale by the tail with the fishing pole. After catching it, they can identify the letter on it.

Variations Print numerals, sight words, or math facts on the whales.

Reproducible Page

Shop and Save

Coupons can be used for sorting, numeral recognition, addition, and multiplication.

Materials
- ☐ coupons from newspapers and store advertisements
- ☐ lunch sacks
- ☐ scissors, markers
- ☐ coupon pouch or billfold

Directions Ask children to cut out coupons from the newspapers and advertisements. Print corresponding values in cents on the lunch sacks as shown. Have children take the coupons and sort them into the appropriate sacks. Store the coupons in a pouch or billfold.

Variations Sort coupons into different categories, such as "foods" and "non-foods."

Ask older children to add the coupons to see how much money they could save. How much would they save if it were double coupon day?

Give children a certain amount of money to spend on food for their family for a week; have them look at a grocery store advertisement and make a shopping list.

Use menus from restaurants for children to see what they could order for a specified amount.

Flip Flop

Children won't realize they are learning letters, numerals, and other skills as they flip these burgers.

Materials
- ☐ poster board
- ☐ scissors, markers
- ☐ spatula

Directions Cut out hamburgers from the poster board using the pattern below. On the front of each hamburger, write a math expression like "2 + 3." On the back, write the answer. Children lay out the hamburgers on the floor or a table. They read the problem and say the answer, and then take the spatula and flip over the hamburger to see if they are correct.

Variations Use this game for identifying upper- and lowercase letters, sets, numerals, beginning sounds, alphabetical order, antonyms, and other skills.

Use this game to reinforce phonics and phonemic awareness skills.

 **Reproducible Page**

Face Graphing

This activity will provide children with a very concrete way to graph and make comparisons.

Materials
☐ paper plates
☐ crayons, markers
☐ bulletin board paper

Directions
Ask each child to decorate his paper plate to look like his face. Place two large sheets of bulletin board paper on the floor. On the top of one, write the word "cats" and draw a cat. On the other, write the word "dogs" and draw a dog. Have children sit on the floor with their paper-plate faces. Ask them to decide which animal is their favorite between a cat and a dog; then have each one place his paper-plate face under the appropriate picture. When all the children have placed their plates, ask them which category has more. Count the plates on both sides to verify their guess. Use the plate faces for other comparisons, such as their favorite food, how many people are in their family, how many teeth they've lost, their favorite color, their favorite character in a story, and so forth.

Variations
Have children make smaller faces on 2" circles to use on a graph made on a piece of poster board.

Use leaves, blocks, crayons, and other common objects to make graphs.

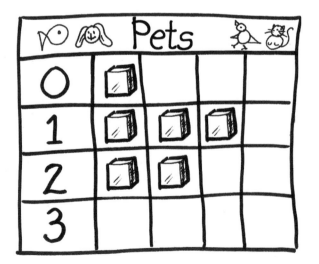

Let's Go to School

(A Community Board Game)

Map making and community pride are enhanced with a board game that reflects the children's neighborhood.

Materials
- ☐ poster board
- ☐ markers, crayons
- ☐ small toy animals
- ☐ 1 die or a pair of dice

Directions Involve children in making a map of their school community. Small groups of children might do this in the block center, on the board, or on large pieces of newsprint. Incorporate children's ideas of the important places in their neighborhood in drawing a board game, similar to the one below, on the poster board. Let children decorate it with markers or crayons.

To play the game, each child chooses an animal and puts it on "Home." Children take turns rolling the dice and moving their animal that number of spaces. The first one to reach the school wins.

Variations Divide older children into groups and let them make their own community board games.

Incorporate math and reading flash cards into the game.

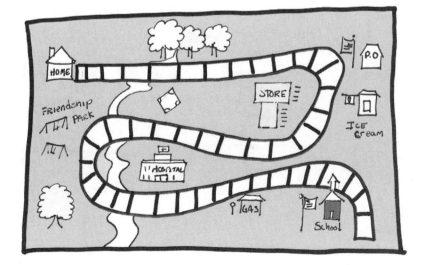

Word Hunt

Sight words will be easy to learn with this word hunt.

Materials
- ☐ sentence strips or index cards
- ☐ marker or crayon
- ☐ tape
- ☐ pointer (yardstick, paper wand, etc.)

Directions
Choose five sight words you would like children to learn. Write each sight word on five index cards or sentence strips. Tape four copies of each word around the room on the walls, cabinets, windows, door, ceiling, etc. Gather children and ask them if they've seen some words hidden around the room. Hold up one word at a time and read it together with the children. Tell children to raise their hands if they can find that same word hidden in the room. Let children have turns taking the pointer and finding the word in the room. Encourage them to read the word as they point to it. Continue finding other hidden words.

Variations
Hide spelling words for children to find each week.

Make a list of words found in the classroom and photocopy it. Children can put the list on a clipboard, go around the room, and check off the words as they find them.

Let children go on a "letter hunt" or "numeral hunt" by finding different letters and numerals in the classroom and pointing to them.

Cut out a star pattern from construction paper and staple it to a straw to make a pointer.

Piece of Pie

A pizza pie is good to eat, but it can also be a clever learning tool for children.

Materials
☐ round cardboard from pizza
☐ markers, ruler
☐ clothespins (spring-type)

Directions
Divide the pizza cardboard into eight pie shapes. Color each section a different color. Color eight clothespins corresponding colors. Have children clip clothespins onto the appropriate colors.

Variations
Write color words on the clothespins for children to match.

Put different sets of sausages (small red circles) on the pie shapes and write numerals on the clothespins for children to match.

Print math problems on the pizza slices and write the answers on the clothespins.

Color pizza cardboards to look like pies and cut them into fraction puzzles. Label similar cardboards as shown so children can match them up.

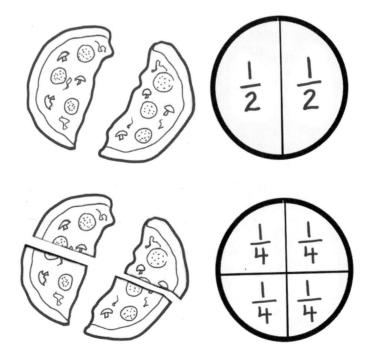

Parts of Speech Bingo

Children will learn to identify parts of speech in a sentence with this adaptation of bingo.

Materials
- ☐ heavy paper cut 6" × 8" and divided into 6 equal sections
- ☐ 3" × 5" index cards
- ☐ markers, scissors
- ☐ box or bag
- ☐ beans or other objects to use as markers

noun	adjective
verb	pronoun
verb	conjunction

Directions
Use a marker to divide each sheet of paper into six equal sections. Write the following parts of speech randomly on the heavy paper in the sections: noun, verb, adjective, adverb, pronoun, conjunction. Some cards should have the same part of speech written twice. These are the bingo cards that children will use to play the game. Distribute the parts of speech cards to children, along with beans or other objects to use as markers.

Write sentences on the index cards. For each sentence, underline the word that shows the part of speech for that card. For example, write "My bicycle is blue." "Blue" is the underlined word, and it is an adjective. Make sure you have at least two sentences for each part of speech.

Put the sentences in a box or bag. Pull out one sentence at a time and hold it up for children to see. Read the sentence aloud, and tell children which word is underlined. If children have the part of speech that matches the underlined word, they cover it up with one of their markers. For the sentence "My bicycle is <u>blue</u>," children find "adjective" on their card and cover it. If a child has two of the same part of speech, she can cover only one at a time. When a child covers all the parts of speech on his card, he yells, "Bingo!" The game continues until each child has covered up all the sections on his card.

Variations
Play a similar game to help children learn their addition facts. Print numbers on the heavy paper; print addition problems on index cards. Children may cover up the numbers on their bingo cards as the corresponding problems are drawn.

Use cereal or crackers as markers, and then let children eat them as a treat.

Memory Games

Memory games are excellent for developing visual memory, reading skills, and attention span.

Materials
☐ poster board cut in 3½" squares
☐ stickers (2 of each)

Directions
Make matching cards by putting like stickers on each pair of squares. Mix up the cards and put them face down on the floor or a table. One child at a time chooses two squares and turns them over. If the stickers match, then that child may keep the pair and have another turn. If they don't match, the child has to turn them over and the next child gets a turn. The game continues until all the pairs of cards have been matched.

Variations
To introduce this game, use four pairs of cards. As children improve, increase the number of pairs used in the game.

Get two of the same toy catalogs or store advertisements and cut out matching objects to use in making memory cards. Coupons, food labels, and logos also make interesting memory games.

Use Old Maid cards to play memory games.

Make memory games in which children must match up sight words, upper- and lowercase letters, sets and numerals, or like shapes.

Make memory games in which children must match antonyms, synonyms, a part of speech with a word that matches that part of speech, shape words with their shapes, and sums with addition problems.

Movable Alphabet

With these letter blocks children will see how letters can be put together to build words, and how words can be put together to build sentences.

Materials
- [ ] unit blocks
- [ ] tagboard
- [ ] tape, scissors, markers

Directions   Cut the tagboard into 2½" squares to fit on the smallest unit blocks. Write alphabet letters on the squares, and tape one onto each block. (Make two of letters frequently used, such as *a, e, i, o, l, s, t*.) Demonstrate how you can take the letter blocks and put them together to "build" words. Encourage children to make the individual sound of the letter on each block, and then blend the sounds together to read the words.

Variations   Make word families that children can read by changing the first letter in words such as *can, run, pot, like, make, pin, town, bat, pet, run*, etc.

Let children use these blocks to make spelling words or vocabulary words.

Cut the tagboard into 2½" × 5" rectangles and write sight words on them. Tape these to larger unit blocks. Put the word blocks together to build sentences that children can read.

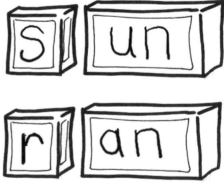

Doughnut Holes

You can't eat these doughnuts, but children will enjoy playing with them just the same.

Materials
- [ ] construction paper
- [ ] scissors, markers
- [ ] plastic zipper bag

Directions   Cut out ten doughnuts and holes using the patterns below. On each doughnut, write a number word. On each hole, write a matching numeral. Children take the doughnut holes and match them up to the appropriate doughnut. Store the doughnuts and holes in a plastic zipper bag.

Variations   Put dots (chocolate chips) on the doughnuts and matching numerals on the holes.

Use this format for matching upper- and lowercase letters.

For younger children, cut doughnuts out of different kinds of wallpaper and have them match up like patterns.

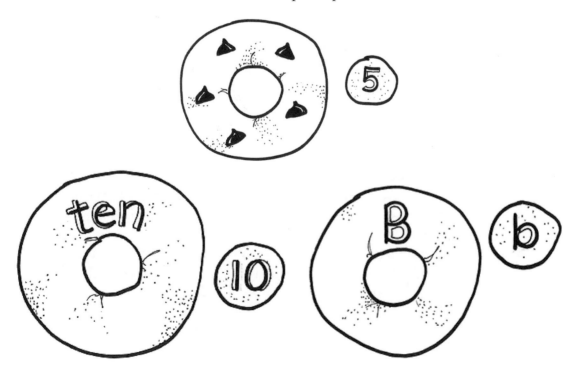

 **Reproducible Page**

Doodle Bug

This game can reinforce math and reading skills, while children use their small motor skills in a creative way.

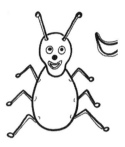

Materials
- ☐ poster board cut to 14" × 10"
- ☐ copy of the game board from the following page
- ☐ glue
- ☐ paper, pencils
- ☐ heavy paper cut in 2½" × 4" rectangles (25)
- ☐ caps from dried-up magic markers

Directions Glue the game board on the following page onto the poster board. On the rectangular cards, write sight words, math problems, letters, or other facts. Also make one, two, or three dots on each card as shown. Players choose a magic marker cap and put it on "Start." Each player will also need a pencil and a piece of paper.

Shuffle the cards and put them face down in the middle of the board. One at a time, children draw a card and identify the information on it. They may then move their marker the number of dots indicated on the card and draw that body part for their "doodlebug." (They must have the head or body before they can draw the legs and other features. If they can't use the body part they land on, then they must wait until their next turn to draw.) Children continue moving around the game board until they have completed drawing their "doodlebugs." (When all the cards have been drawn from the center of the board, shuffle them up and begin again.)

Variation For older children, write questions on the cards that relate to a unit of study, current events, or literature that they have read.

STEP IT UP Have children read books about insects. When children play the game, have them draw a specific kind of insect and label their drawings with the name of the insect. You may need to modify the board so children do not need to draw really tiny features, or features that real insects do not have.

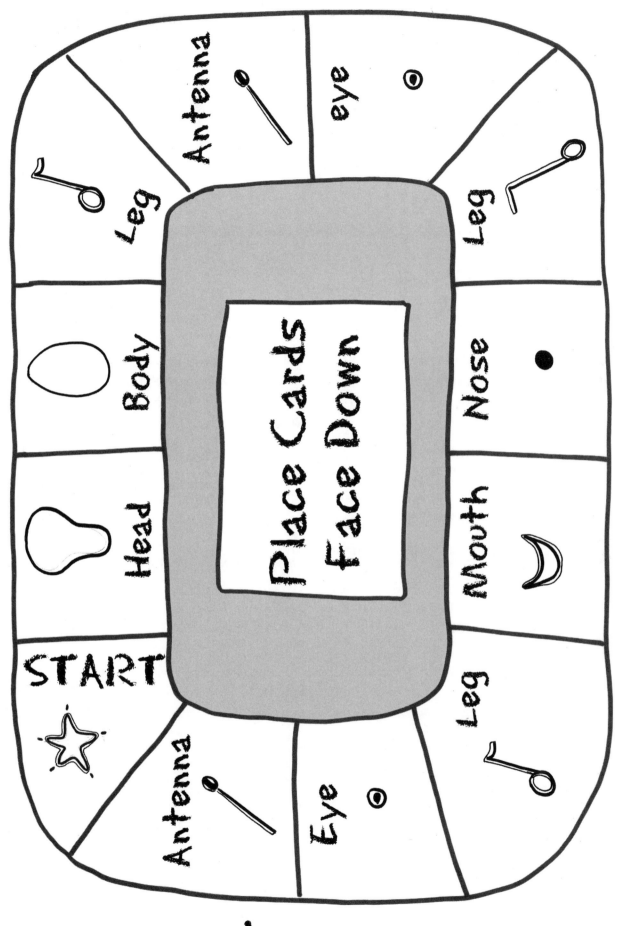

Addition and Subtraction Dice

This game is a fun way to practice addition and subtraction facts to 50.

Materials
☐ 2 six-sided dice
☐ paper, pencils

Directions
Divide the class into pairs. Give each pair two dice. One child rolls the dice and writes an addition problem based on the numbers on the dice. For example: 3 + 4 = 7. Then the child's partner takes a turn. Children continue taking turns until each child's answers add up to 50 (or more). The first child of the pair to reach 50 is the winner.

Do a reversal of this game with subtraction. Children start with 50. They roll the dice and subtract the smaller number from the larger number. For example: 5 – 3 = 2. They subtract the difference from 50. The first child to get to 0 is the winner.

Variation
Use sums and differences to 100.

Show Time

Show Time encourages children to focus on skills, and can be a valuable tool for teachers to use in assessment.

Materials
- ☐ 3" × 5" index cards
- ☐ envelopes
- ☐ markers

Directions Make a set of numeral cards for each child by writing the numerals from 0 to 10 on the index cards (one numeral on each card). Have each child put her numeral cards in an envelope and print her name on the front. To play "Show Time," ask children to lay out their cards in front of them. Tell them to hold up different numerals as you call them out. (This enables you to quickly observe children who are weak in this area.) You can also snap your fingers or clap a certain number of times, and ask children to hold up the appropriate numeral.

Variations To reinforce addition and subtraction, call out a part of a math fact and have children hold up the answer.

Make up word problems and ask children to "show" you the answer.

For younger children, start with the numerals 1 to 5. For older children, use higher numbers.

To review consonant sounds, print letters on index cards and have children hold up the sound they hear when you call out different words.

Where Is Mousie?

Mousie can hide under letters, numerals, or words, which children learn as they look for him.

Materials
☐ poster board cut in 8" squares
☐ gray construction paper
☐ scissors, markers

Directions
Cut out a small mouse from the construction paper using the pattern below. On the poster board, print sight words. Have children sit on the floor in a circle. Ask them to read the words as you place them on the floor in the middle of the circle. Tell children to turn around and close their eyes as you hide Mousie under one of the words. When children turn back around, repeat this chant:

> *Mousie, Mousie, where can you be?*
> *Mousie, Mousie, let's peek and see!*

Choose one child to guess where Mousie is hiding. The child says the word, and then peeks under it to see if Mousie is there. The game continues until someone finds the mouse. That person may then hide Mousie.

Variation
Print numerals, letters, different shapes, or other information on the cards. Make a paper turkey, jack-o'-lantern, snowflake, heart, or other symbol to relate to a season or holiday to hide under the cards.

🚶 **Reproducible Page**

Alligator

Don't let the alligator catch you not paying attention in this game!

Materials
- ☐ can with a smooth edge (potato stick and drink mix cans work well)
- ☐ white poster board cut in 5" × 2" rectangles
- ☐ markers, scissors, glue
- ☐ green construction paper

Directions
Cut 30 rectangles from the poster board. Print the letters of the alphabet on the bottom of 26 of them. On the other four, draw a small alligator similar to the one at the bottom of the page. Cover the can with green construction paper and "alligator eyes," as shown. Mix up the cards; then put them all in the can. (The letter end of each card should be placed in the bottom of the can.) Explain that you will pass the alligator can around and everyone can draw out a card. If they get a card with a letter, they should say the name of the letter. If they get an alligator, they should yell, "Alligator," and everyone else must stand up and run in place. Start the game with this rhyme:

> *There's a big, bad alligator sneaking up on you,*
> *And he's going to take a bite if you don't know what to do.*
> *So open up your eyes and ears and do what I say.*
> *Are you ready? Get set! Let's play!*

Continue playing the game until all the cards have been drawn. Mix them up and begin all over again.

Variations
Have children think of words that begin with the letters they draw.

Draw shapes or colors on the cards for younger children, and write numerals, math facts, and sight words for older children.

Change the game so whoever draws the alligator is "out" of the game. The last one left wins.

Quiz Time

This simple game can be used for reinforcing many concepts, and can be adapted to different skill levels.

Materials
- ☐ 3" × 5" index cards
- ☐ golf tees
- ☐ hole punch
- ☐ fine-tip markers
- ☐ zipper bag

Directions Write different math expressions on the index cards. On the bottom, write three possible answers and punch a hole under each numeral as shown. On the back side, draw a circle around the correct response. Each child takes an index card and a golf tee. The child inserts the golf tee into the hole next to the answer she chooses. The child can then turn the card over to check her answer. Store the cards and golf tees in a zipper bag.

Variation Make similar games for alphabetical order, numerical order, sets and numerals, sight words, or initial consonant sounds. Older children can use this game format for a question and answer review.

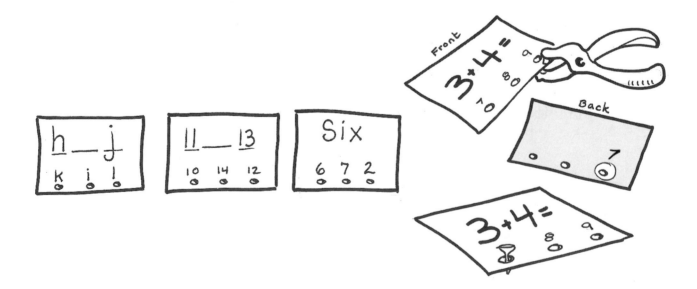

Bean Counters

The bean counter is an effective way to introduce measurement to children.

Materials
- ☐ large lima beans
- ☐ clear packaging tape

Directions Lay out a piece of packaging tape (approximately 10" long), sticky side up on the table. Place ten beans side by side in the middle of the tape as shown. Fold both sides of the tape over the beans. Seal the ends and trim. Let children use the bean counter to measure "how many beans long" various objects are. Challenge children to find something three beans long or seven beans long. Ask them what they could do if they wanted to measure something longer than their bean counter.

Variations Use bean counters to practice counting by tens or to introduce place value.

Make similar counters out of pasta, foam peanuts, and other flat objects.

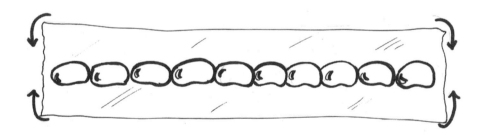

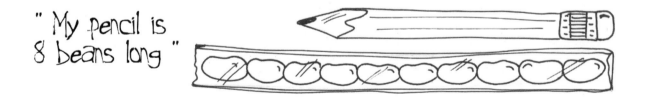

" My pencil is 8 beans long "

Scrambled Words

Here's a partner game in which children will need to work together to figure out scrambled words before the other teams.

Materials
- ☐ sentence strips, each with a scrambled word written on it
- ☐ wipe-off boards
- ☐ dry-erase markers

Directions Divide the class into pairs. Each pair is a team. Display a sentence strip with a word on it that has all of the letters mixed up. Have each pair work together to unscramble the word. Have children work through their ideas on the wipe-off boards. When time is up, children must circle the word that is their final answer. Teams show their boards to the class. Each team that circled the correct word earns a point. The team that has the most points when you end the game wins.

Tangrams

Tangrams contribute to an understanding of mathematical concepts as well as problem-solving and motor skills.

Materials
- ☐ tangram shapes (see following page)
- ☐ felt or heavy cardboard
- ☐ scissors
- ☐ index cards

Directions Cut tangram shapes out of felt or heavy cardboard using the patterns on the following page. Draw tangram patterns on index cards for the children to reproduce. Encourage children to explore with the shapes and create their own objects; then put out the patterns for them to copy.

Variation Increase the complexity of the patterns as children become more proficient.

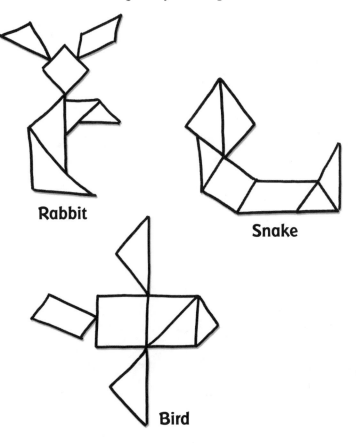

Rabbit

Snake

Bird

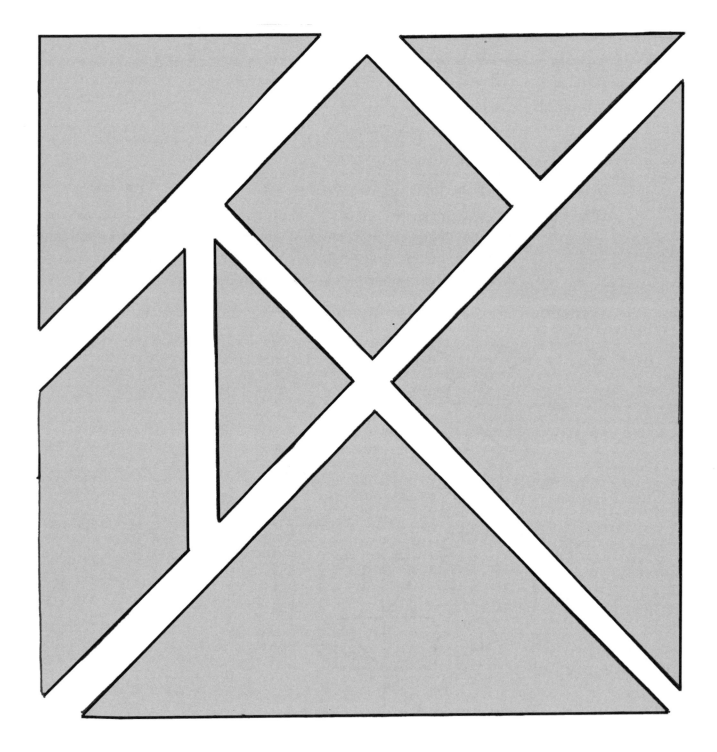

Snake Eyes

Children will be counting and recognizing numerals as they play this game of chance.

Materials
- ☐ 2 dice
- ☐ score card for each child
- ☐ pen or pencil

Directions Give each child a score card like the one shown and a pen or pencil. One at a time, children take turns rolling the dice. They can count the number of dots on each die, and then mark off the resulting numerals on their score cards. The first child to scratch off all of his or her 2s (1 + 1 = snake eyes) wins!

Variation For older children, write numerals from 2 to 12, and then let them add up their dice to mark off numerals on their score cards.

SCORE CARD

1	1	1	1	1	1	1
2	2	2	2	2	2	2
3	3	3	3	3	3	3
4	4	4	4	4	4	4
5	5	5	5	5	5	5
6	6	6	6	6	6	6

Eggs in a Nest

Counting, numeral recognition, sorting, and joining sets can become meaningful with this game.

Materials
- ☐ paper lunch sacks
- ☐ colored pom poms
- ☐ small squares of paper
- ☐ marker

Directions Open the lunch sacks and roll them down as you mold them into nests. Print numerals on the squares of paper and place one in each nest. Have children count out the appropriate number of eggs (pom poms) and place them in each nest.

Variations Ask children to sort the pom poms by color into nests.

Write number words on the nests for children to read and make sets.

Let children join and separate sets with the eggs in the nests.

You can also use cotton balls for eggs, or have children mold their own eggs out of clay or play dough.

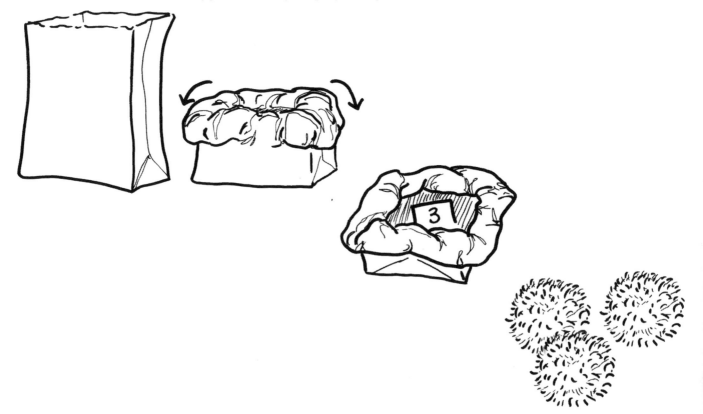

Activities and Ideas Index

W

Z

Materials Index

A

B

C

D

E

F

G

H

I

Common Core State Standards
Addressed by *Wonderful Rooms Where Children Can Bloom!*

Letters and numbers in parentheses represent the grade levels covered by this book for the given standard.

Math

- Count to 100 by ones and by tens. **(K)**

- Write numbers from 0 to 20. Represent a number of objects with a written numeral 0–20 (with 0 representing a count of no objects). **(K)**

- Understand the relationship between numbers and quantities; connect counting to cardinality. **(K)**

- Understand that the three digits of a three-digit number represent amounts of hundreds, tens, and ones. **(1–2)**

- Measure the length of an object by selecting and using appropriate tools. **(K–2)**

- Correctly name shapes regardless of their orientations or overall size. **(K)**

- Model shapes in the world by building shapes from components and drawing shapes. **(K–2)**

Reading/Language Arts

- Describe characters, settings, and major events in a story, using key details. **(K–2)**

- Demonstrate understanding of the organization and basic features of print. **(K–1)**

- Know and apply grade-level phonics and word analysis skills in decoding words. **(K–2)**

- Participate in shared research and writing projects. **(K–2)**

- Participate in collaborative conversations with diverse partners with peers and adults in small and larger groups. **(K–2)**

- Add drawings or other visual displays to descriptions when appropriate to clarify ideas, thoughts, and feelings. **(K–2)**

- Demonstrate command of the conventions of standard English grammar and usage when writing or speaking. **(K–2)**

- Demonstrate command of the conventions of standard English capitalization, punctuation, and spelling when writing. **(K–2)**

- Use words and phrases acquired through conversations, reading and being read to, and responding to texts. **(K–2)**